'... that is what we do – we go out and destroy other people's lives.'
Former news editor on the *News of the World*

'We shouldn't be writing about anybody's private life at all unless there is some really powerful public need to know about it.'
Nick Davies, *Flat Earth News*

NEWS OF THE WORLD?

FAKE SHEIKHS & ROYAL TRAPPINGS

PETER BURDEN

NEWS OF THE WORLD?
FAKE SHEIKHS & ROYAL TRAPPINGS

Published by

Eye Books

Challenging the way we see things

News of the world? Fake Sheikhs & Royal Trappings
First Edition

Published by Eye Books Ltd 2008
8 Peacock Yard
Iliffe Street
London
SE17 3LH

Tel. +44 (0) 845 450 8870
Email: info@eye-books.com
Website: www.eye-books.com

Typeset in Minion Pro and Bureau Grotesque

ISBN-10: 1-903070-79-1 (HB)
ISBN-13: 978-1-903070-79-6 (HB)

Printed and bound in Great Britain by Cromwell Press, Trowbridge, Wiltshire

I feel strongly that there is a need for people to stand up for their beliefs. Part of the philosophy of Eye Books is to champion things that empower the underdog in this increasingly celebrity driven, mechanized world in which we live.

Like most people I have a thirst for gossip and sensationalism. So I feel the need for a balance in the stories we are increasingly 'drip-fed' which inevitably influence our judgment. I want a media that acts as a positive rather than a negative influence and empowers the individual to care and make a difference as opposed to one which revels in others misfortunes.

Having published Waseem's (the brother of the News of the World's infamous Fake Sheikh) book - Good Morning Afghanistan, I heard myself repeat the marketing slogan we employed: at the time: 'Waseem uses media to rebuild people's lives whilst his brother uses media to destroy them'

This was what I/Eye wanted to champion.

Little did I know that a previously twice-published Eye Books author would come knocking with a manuscript which championed this message and addressed the growing gap between what media define to be 'in' the public interest and 'of' public interest.

This confusion with what is 'of' public interest instead of 'in' the public interest leads to negative reporting. With a clear definition of 'of', the need for a greater balance could be enforced. It is down to the relevant bodies to recognise this issue and frame effective privacy laws.

'News of the world?' is different to most of our other books; in some ways it highlights the negatives instead of pushing forward the positives. However, I feel it fits with the important message that we as individuals have to care about the mismanagement of standards and care about the lengths the media are able to go to simply for their own needs rather than for a wider good.

Much of our (Eye Books) message has arguably been too implicit in previous books. Most media enjoys being explicit. With this book we have decided to unveil those who revel in exposing their subjects in the hope that perhaps us all wearing the other shoe can see how it fits when it's on the other foot.

Dan Hiscocks
Publisher Eye-Books

www.eye-books.com

1. Everyone has the right to respect for his private and family life, his home and his correspondence.

2. There shall be no interference by a public authority with the exercise of this right except such as is in accordance with the law and is necessary in a democratic society in the interests of national security, public safety or the economic well-being of the country, for the prevention of disorder or crime, for the protection of health or morals, or for the protection of the rights and freedoms of others.

The European Convention on Human Rights – Article 8

Acknowledgements

I am grateful for the help and advice of Matthew Engel, Roy Greenslade, John Harris, Sir Simon Jenkins, Tim Toulmin, John Whittingdale MP, Ron Mackay, Waseem Mahmood, Max Clifford, and all those who, sympathetic to my cause, have allowed me close enough to overhear their treacherous murmurings.

CONTENTS

FOREWORD

This is not a textbook for journalists. It is intended to explain in layman's terms the anarchy that has developed in some sectors of the British Press. It sets out to be an accurate and dispassionate examination of slovenliness and malpractice in British journalism which in any other profession would be exposed and brought to face justice. There is a growing body of opinion that newspapers like the News of the World – by no means the only culprit – are out of control and unaccountable.

The "Red Tops" – bright-bannered and branded with outsize, eye-grabbing headlines – are operating beyond the law because the bodies and statutes in place whose function it is to protect the innocent and the privacy of both public and private individuals are too weak to achieve a balanced restraint.

Like many members of the public, I am alarmed that after the recent explosion in communications and unprecedented free flow of information around the globe, both truth and privacy appear to be more vulnerable than ever. I am not a journalist, nor have I ever been, thus I am not a member of a journalistic freemasonry which tends – with no doubt honourable intentions – to protect its fellows from each other. For the sake of clarity I have focused on the activities of one newspaper over recent years in the hope of encouraging those who legislate on the workings of our national press to revisit the bases on which it is monitored and contained.

THE HACK AND THE HACKER

November, 2005

Late afternoon sun brightened the pale stone of Hawksmoor's handsome church of St George and glinted on the triangular cap of Canary Wharf a couple of miles to the east. It gleamed, too, off the sleek, black hair of a thickset, middle-aged man walking past the gates of the leaf-strewn churchyard. As he strode briskly across The Highway in Wapping, the Saturday afternoon traffic was light, and a breeze rippled the last few leaves on the plane trees that edged the broad thoroughfare.

The dapper, pin-striped figure reached the south side where the usual hubbub of football on the widescreen and raucous amateur commentary spilled from the corner door of The Old Rose. Among the crowd of drinkers that had replaced the dockworkers who once filled the bars were several newsroom colleagues, journalists who had already filed their stories for the next issues of the two mighty Sunday newspapers – the *News of the World* and *The Sunday Times* – which in a few hours would explode from the converted tobacco warehouse on the cobbled street behind the old East London pub.

The former warehouse, now a fortress of tinted glass and concrete thrust up from the Victorian dockside building, is the British hub of News International, one of the largest and most powerful media conglomerates in the world, largely owned and entirely controlled by Australian-born media mogul, Keith Rupert Murdoch.

Murdoch is widely considered to be one of the most controversial newspaper owners the world has ever known. A brilliant and ruthless business strategist, unrestrained by political or ideological loyalties, over the years he has shown the world his willingness to take commercial gambles on a mind-numbing scale, brazenly changing political horses and editorial direction without a qualm to suit his current trading priorities. His editors are well aware that on a Murdoch paper the needs of the bottom line are generally expected to out-trump journalistic integrity.

Amid an atmosphere of high angst that pervades the Wapping news-bunker, this ethos is clearly transmitted to every writer on the staff – as is Murdoch's staunch republican point of view. When it comes to reporting on the Royal Family, Murdoch's anti-monarchist stance encourages little restraint. At times, this cynical, hardening process has had the effect of pushing journalists right to the edge – sometimes beyond.

Clive Goodman checked the time on the fob watch that hung from the chunky gold chain adorning his double-breasted waistcoat, and pressed on. He had one last phone call to make, a call which might, if he was very lucky, provide him with something to bulk out his regular column. It wouldn't have taken much to improve it, so flimsy was that week's offering. He winced nervously, keenly aware of the meagreness of his contribution in what had turned out to be a slender week for the *News of the World*.

The front-page splash, "WHY I BEAT ENDER LOVER" – the tale of soap "star" Steve McFadden assaulting his woman – was about as thin as it got.

And, bannered above, "KERRY IS DUMPED BY FIANCÉ."

News?

Of the World?

No wonder the more cynical members of the public had long called the paper the *"News of the Screws"* – or more succinctly, the *"Screws"*. What made it worse for Goodman was that within the small journalistic niche he occupied – chronicling the lives of the Royal Family – were three other royal-related stories, all of which appeared in the paper ahead of his own column on page 32, and none of which carried his by-line.

Mark Bolland, former royal hired hand and sycophant who'd made it clear that Goodman didn't impress him, had a sniping little piece about Camilla's hair and make-up, while new, thrusting young royal reporter Ryan Sabey had written about Charles and Camilla inspecting the aftermath of Hurricane Katrina in Louisiana, above a small item which claimed that Prince Harry didn't want Camilla to come with his father to the "Parents' Evening" at Sandhurst, the military academy where he was training to be an army officer. A snippet, no doubt, Clive thought bitterly, from one of Bolland's chums at Clarence House.

Goodman gloomily reviewed the scrappy titbits he had so far assembled for his quarter of page 32:

The first involved Prince Charles meeting top British hack Tina Brown at a reception in New York, where he asked her if she was "still journalising". The Prince obviously didn't know (which everyone in publishing did) that she had already started yet another biography of the late Princess Diana.

The second was about an unnamed singer in an unnamed band, who, on being complimented for his playing by an unidentified other party, replied, "I ain't no Picasso".

In the final, not very juicy morsel, Peter Mandelson sits down to lunch with Derek Draper and, for reasons that are unclear, leaves in a huff before the first course arrives.

By no stretch of the imagination, Goodman realised, could any of this be described as heady stuff – not what his readers, even the not very discerning ones, expected from "Blackadder, your snake in the grass of the rich and powerful", as his column was billed. But he had nothing else. He had raked through his list of contacts, former reliable and consistent sources. He had called Nigel Pollitzer, a regular supplier of society gossip in former times and admitted he was desperate. 'Have you got anything – anything will do?'

But most of those he called, if they didn't simply reject his calls, told him politely – sometimes not so politely – that they hadn't got a thing, and these were people he'd lunched frequently and liberally at Langan's fashionable bistro over years of his career. He was beginning to feel so past his use-by date he could have wept with frustration. He walked in through the gates, past the tight security of Rupert Murdoch's defences at News International, Wapping and made his way up to his corner of the newsroom.

His desk phone rang.

He prayed it was his own 'private' snooper, earning the very generous retainer Clive had been paying him – £500 a week, in cash. On the basis of his former track record, Clive was able to claim it on his expenses, as payment to 'Alexander' for services researching royal stories.

In an anonymous building in a small commercial estate in Sutton on the south west fringes of London, 'Alexander', who didn't know Clive's code name for him although he regularly operated under aliases of his own, listened to Goodman's voice wheezing down the line. A faint grimace spread across his clean-cut young features. There were times when he really didn't like his job. Still, no one would be hurt, no property damaged. And the money was good.

'I've done it,' he said. 'I'll just check it and text you.'

In Wapping, Clive listened, grunted his thanks and put the phone down to wait for the follow-up call. Less than two minutes later, his mobile bleeped the arrival of a text message. Goodman retrieved it and jotted down the four numbers it contained. With the slight tremor of fear and guilt he always felt when he made calls like this, he picked up his landline phone, punched a number, waited, and entered the PIN which 'Alexander' said would connect him remotely to his target's voicemail. Goodman heard the announcement that there were new messages waiting, caught his breath and stabbed '1' with a doughy finger. He listened for ten or fifteen seconds while a satisfied smile spread across his pale lips, hit "1" again for a second listen, and began scribbling on his notepad. He put the phone down with a long sigh of relief. These fishing expeditions so often yielded nothing, but this time, he had his lead story. It didn't quite live up to the strap that used to adorn his column, "Behind the Big Stories", but at least his billet in the newsroom was safe for a little while longer.

It wasn't unusual for investigative journalists (including royal watchers) to engage the services of private investigators or specialist information gatherers, but Goodman had his own particular arrangement with this PI. 'Alexander' was in reality 34-year-old ex-AFC Wimbledon footballer Glenn 'Trigger' Mulcaire, AKA Paul Williams and John Jenkins. Officially, Mulcaire was employed by News International as a free-lance to provide 'research and information services' – tracing car numbers, finding ex-directory phone numbers, checking credit-ratings – all ordinary requirements of the kind of investigative journalism Clive practised.

Good-looking, intelligent, ambitious and resourceful, since his earlier football career had come to an end, Glenn had sought an interesting way of earning a decent living. He'd got into the surveillance business, gathering information in all of the legitimate ways that were available for a variety of commercial and media organisations. One of his biggest clients was News International, and his main contact there, Greg Miskiw, had become a friend.

Miskiw, who was then working on the news desk at the *News of the World*, suggested Glenn form a company that would work exclusively for News International, providing a wide variety of research services for some of the journalists on his paper. Such jobs included those the hacks themselves either didn't have the time or couldn't be seen to be doing; some of them required particular technical skills and knowledge in which Glenn had trained himself and at which he had become very adept. Glenn was aware that some of the things investigators were asked to do lay in the grey margin between what was legal and what was not, but they didn't involve theft, violence or drugs, and there were no victims in the traditional sense of the word. In any case, Greg explained, most of what Glenn would be asked to do would be to corroborate (or debunk) stories already in place.

Mulcaire decided to go for it. As the father of five children, he appreciated the potential for high earnings that hard work could bring. He was already adept at the art of "blagging" – impersonating a fellow employee over the phone to acquire personal information from banks or NHS data centres or to give 'internal' instructions to mobile phone companies. Blagging is a comparatively simple process and even in a highly technical field it is one of the quickest ways to get a result – if you're good at it. Beyond that, Glenn had already developed contacts inside the relevant industries and skills in other surveillance techniques as his services were used more and more frequently by News International's top Sunday paper.

At Greg Miskiw's urging, Mulcaire started a small company, Nine Consultancy, which claimed, in a spirit of irony perhaps, to protect its clients from unwanted technical intrusion of various sorts. He was soon billing over £100,000 pa to News International alone.

While some of the services he offered were standard legal investigative practices, he was aware that others strayed close to the edge. In the guise of 'Alexander', he had come to his arrangement with Goodman in early 2006 whereby the journalist would pay him £500 a week, in cash, in return for first look at anything that might suit the "Blackadder" column, with special emphasis on royal stories. This cash sum was paid in addition to Mulcaire's £2,000-a-week retainer from News International, presumably so that the bosses at the *News of the World* wouldn't need to know what was going on (which would prove to be their unassailable defence when these activities came to be examined in court.)

Methods such as these were not rare in the field of investigative and celebrity journalism. Known in the trade as the "dark arts", they'd been one of Fleet Street's naughty secrets for some time. It's surprising that until 2006 when the Information Commissioner's Office carried out a detailed investigation, the question of how journalists tracked down people's home addresses and telephone numbers rarely got an airing in the press, possibly because it's a grubby matter, like an antisocial habit in which all the papers – even broadsheets of the highest brow – have to indulge from time to time, and are reluctant to discuss.

In Britain finding a person's home address using perfectly legitimate means is relatively easy, and a number of sources allow journalists to do this as well. If a target is known to be a company director, he or she will be registered at Companies House. Along with the name will be a date of birth and a home address, as well as the company's financial status and performance. Only in exceptional cases will a director not list a home address, which he or she is required by law to do. All of these details are listed online on the Companies House website and can be accessed in minutes for a small fee.

A second useful tool is the electoral role. By law, everybody eligible to vote in Britain must be registered as a voter. The role is available for inspection by anybody in public libraries throughout the country. It is an invaluable resource which can throw up other useful information, like whether or not an individual has a wife or children (of voting age).

Also available for a few pounds is access to the nation's registry of births, deaths and marriages, which can be scrutinised on microfilm at larger city libraries. August 2004 saw the launch of a company called Tracesmart through whom the whole thing can be done online at 15p a throw. The company says it provides 'both corporate clients and private customers with a powerful people tracing solution.' With a database of over 70 million names along with every one of the UK's 29 million addresses, they've been so successful they've already had to move twice to larger premises.

Another weapon in the journalist's armoury, although now a little rusty, is the good old phone book (or, better, BT's online directory). Once the main source of information, the phone book is less useful these days, both because most people in the public eye have their numbers listed as ex-directory and because many of the rest find they can manage more cheaply with a mobile and no land line.

Other legitimate sources used by the media, particularly the tabloid press, include the Land Registry, which can tell a reporter who owns the property at a particular address. The Land Registry can also be accessed on line in the blink of an eye for as little as £3.

Old-fashioned legwork can still produce results, too. If someone famous lives in a town, most (though by no means all) of the locals will know where and will point a journalist in the right direction. And having found their target, some investigators have achieved spectacular results using the crudest of methods – the study of the contents of an individual's dustbins, a practice now known as 'binology'. When a black plastic bag has been left out in the street or by a back door for the local council contractors to collect it, another party can easily remove the bag and take it elsewhere to rifle through the contents. Any scribbled notes, bank statements, medical prescriptions or letters that haven't been shredded could contain highly sensitive, accessible material. Some operators have had remarkable results by specialising in this practice.

Most of these methods of obtaining information are perfectly legal and used by a wide range of organisations. The trouble is that, for a tabloid journalist in hot pursuit of the best line for his story, they're often not current enough or are too time-consuming. This is where the 'dark arts' come in. As his career had progressed Glenn Mulcaire had made himself familiar with these 'dark arts' and by the time he joined the *News of the World*, there were already a number of PIs like him – shadowy figures who over the years have lent an enormous helping hand to the tabloids. They had also become rich from their work, as Mulcaire's earnings from the *News of the World* suggest. They were well aware how valuable the information they obtained could be in helping the tabloids cut corners, and they would charge accordingly.

It's impossible to estimate accurately how many PIs were engaged in these dark arts by the time Goodman's activities came to light, although several journalists claimed at the time that dozens of recent exclusives had come from illegal tapping.

Of course, no official records exist of how journalists first came across and used these shady operators, and how the need, the practice and the technology evolved. There is an early story of a seasoned hack, drinking in a bar near the Old Bailey, who got into conversation with an ex-policeman. It didn't take long for them to realise there was a lot they could do to help each other, thus laying the foundations for the business Glenn Mulcaire found himself in. Whatever the origins of these practices, by the late 1980s competition for the big stories had become intense and, once it became clear how useful the PIs could be, it seemed that everyone followed suit; and the Information Commissioner's enquiry revealed that one of the PIs investigated was found to have over 350 journalists on his books.

Only the journalists at the coalface dealt with these investigators, never the editors or senior executives, in whose eyes these people never officially existed. But when the hacks' invoices came in for 'research services', they were signed off with no questions asked – in the case of the *News of the World*, by long-standing managing editor Stuart Kuttner. A tacit agreement prevailed that those at the top of a paper's management didn't need to know how their reporters obtained information and the reporters never discussed it with their bosses. If the subject cropped up, hacks were told, 'I don't want to know.'

In a busy tabloid newsroom a junior journalist would probably wait a few years before a senior colleague handed him the number of a man 'who might be able to help you with this.' Meanwhile, the reporters didn't admit to their use of PIs when they talked among themselves in the newsroom, and when they did contact one, they did so as discreetly as possible. For a lazy journalist, it was an attractive option – he could hire a PI to do all the work before even trying legally to find the details for himself. If asked whether they knew how the inquiry agents got their information, most tabloid hacks will shake their heads.

'I'd my suspicions,' one told me, 'but I never asked questions. No one did. You'd make the call to the PI and two hours later you'd have the information. It was as simple as that.'

Glenn Mulcaire had shown himself to be one of the best, which was what had prompted Greg Miskiw to get him on a full time contract with News International, and he was able to raise his fees progressively until they reached £2,000 a week. Glenn was also proving invaluable, almost addictively useful in Clive Goodman's hunger for exclusive scoops, unobtainable to the rest of the pack of royal newshounds. The scam wasn't complicated. Clive had managed to obtain the mobile phone numbers for several members of the Clarence House staff and ultimately of the princes themselves. It was a simple matter for Glenn to pose as a credit control employee and call the target's mobile carrier to get his or her voicemail PIN number changed back to default. Once set to default, he and Goodman were able to browse the private voicemails of such figures as William and Harry's private secretary and Prince Charles's communications secretary. When this all came to light, Goodman and Mulcaire were found to have hacked into their victims' voicemails at least 609 times between them.

Clive must have been very excited – and very relieved – when he discovered that Glenn's voicemail interception worked. Suddenly he was privy to items of personal information on the young Royals that none of his competitors could possibly know. It worked so well he asked Glenn to extend the system to cover a far wider range of newsworthy individuals and soon voicemail hacking became the primary source of Goodman's exclusive royal stories.

CHAPTER ONE

A PRINCE'S KNEE

On November 6, 2005, a small item appeared in the *News of the World* at the top of Clive Goodman's "Blackadder" column, which, insignificant though it was, set in motion a series of events that were to make legal history and send shockwaves through the world's media.

It wasn't a big piece – not a major story; not really news at all – but a snippet of personal, private tittle-tattle that may have pleased the many readers who were ready to gobble up every tiny morsel of the intimate lives of the British Royal Family.

Royal action man Prince William has had to postpone a mountain rescue course – after being crocked by a ten-year-old during football training. William pulled a tendon in his knee after last week's kids' kickabout with Premiership club Charlton Athletic.

Now medics have put him on the sick list. "He has to wear a knee brace if he wants to do anything other than walk, to stop it getting any worse," confided one friend.

The Prince took part in the session in his new role as president elect of the FA.

He has seen Prince Charles's personal doc and is now having physiotherapy at Cirencester hospital, near his county home Highgrove.

"The really important thing is that his leg heals before he starts at Sandhurst in January," said his pal. "He doesn't want to inherit Prince Harry's nickname, Sicknote."

The story was innocuous enough; but it should not, under any circumstances, have been there. Essentially, it was true, unlike the many fabrications about the British Royals that circulated around the world's press. What was less than accurate was the implication of an unnamed "pal" – a term which was no more than a standard, overworked device for adding authenticity to a royal story.

Meanwhile, in Clarence House, home of Prince Charles and his two sons, their staff reviewed the piece from an office overlooking the gold and crimson trees of St James's Park. A few weeks ago, they would have been frustrated and perplexed that this slight story had escaped and drifted across London to settle in the murky air of Wapping. Of the very few people who knew about the Prince's knee, none would have considered talking to anyone about the matter, let alone a member of the press.

But now they had a very good idea of how it had got there.

For several preceding months, stories had been appearing in the News of the World that were causing concern. A careful review of every William or Harry story the paper had published over the previous three years showed that information was leaking, but the idea that a senior member of the Royal Household had been unofficially speaking to the press was unthinkable. Other possible forms of communication had to be considered, particularly email and telephone, although it was unlikely these could be breached, given the security systems in place. Nevertheless, the princes and their staff were warned to be sparing and cautious in their conversations over the phone.

This heightened state of awareness bore fruit, first when Helen Asprey, private secretary to Princes William and Harry, reported a problem. She was regularly left messages about arrangements for events in which members of the Royal Family were to be involved, and she was finding that when she accessed her voicemail, messages which she hadn't previously picked up were listed as 'old', rather than 'new'. Around the same time, the princes' private secretary, Jamie Lowther-Pinkerton, found the same thing happening on his voicemail. It was perhaps possible that he might somehow have relegated one or two messages without hearing them, but it was unlikely. When Paddy Harverson, Prince Charles's press secretary, also reported the same problem, there could be no doubt that there had been a wholesale break into the mobile phones of the Clarence House staff. At first they weren't sure how it was being done, who was doing it and to what extent. However, after Clive Goodman's column had carried a series of stories, all based on voicemail messages left for royal staff, it became clear they had been the victims of 'phone-screwing'. When the 'William's knee' story appeared, discreet enquiries were made within Clarence House to confirm that no other parties might have heard about the injury on which the story was based. It came as no surprise that this produced nothing. At last, all the little stories leaking out to the *News of the World* made sense. The man suspected of being responsible thereby laid himself open to be minutely scrutinised and monitored until he yielded enough evidence to get himself brought to book for gross intrusion into the princes' privacy.

The following week, behind a front-page splash, "GLITTER'S SICK HAREM", the *News of the World* had the usual crop of royal stories dotted about the paper. Young Ryan Sabey had a piece about Poppy Day, and on page 25 Clive Goodman's name appeared above three stories that might all reasonably have been expected to see the light of day. "Wills' battle for Di's millions" reported on the Prince's desire to set up and fund his own office in the manner his father had at his age.

There was a story of a small break in at Prince Charles's Highgrove farm shop, along with a report that the Queen's head of security at Buckingham Palace, Brigadier Jeffrey Cook, had got involved in a wrestling match with the Chinese President's minder. None very elevating stories, but at least more or less true and also in the public domain.

However, on page 40, in another thin edition of Clive Goodman's "Blackadder" column, tucked between a paragraph about Ann Diamond submitting to "Celebrity Fit Club" on ITV (having previously condemned it as 'obesity voyeurism') and a fatuous piece about Chris Evans in the audience at a West End play failing to look at a naked actress, there was a new Prince William story. It was even less momentous than the tale of the twisted knee. But like the last, it could possibly have been known to only three or four people:

If ITN do a stock-take on their portable editing suites this week, they might notice they're one down. That's because their pin-up political editor Tom Bradbury has lent it to close pal Prince William so he can edit together all his gap year videos and DVDs into one very posh home movie.

At least William, who demands to be left in peace by the media can be confident his secret is safe at that rumour-sieve ITN – and that it won't get out and infuriate the BBC. Oops.

At first sight, it wasn't clear what the *News of the World*'s royal editor, Clive Goodman, was implying in his final paragraph – although on the face of it, he was suggesting the leak came from ITN. But why would he want to do that?

However, Clarence House staff were now in no doubt that the appearance of two totally private stories two weeks apart was not a mere coincidence. A meeting was swiftly convened that was to have far-reaching and significant consequences. The Commissioner of the Metropolitan Police was contacted, and he passed instructions to investigate to the anti-terrorist branch of his force.

The two young princes by this stage were trying to get on with their lives with as little disruption from the media as possible. The close involvement of the press – especially the paparazzi – with their mother's death hadn't made it easy, but now they'd accepted a degree of press intrusion as an unavoidable aspect of their royal function, and on the whole they'd handled it well. Prince William had managed to remain a model of discretion despite a fairly comprehensive onslaught by the press. However, after a few years of comparative privacy at St Andrews, he'd had to watch his girlfriend, Kate Middleton, being shamelessly hounded by paparazzi despite all the promises made ten years before by solemn, repentant tabloid editors.

At the time of the phone-tapping, the public perception was that the two young men were fulfilling their function as diligent members of the Armed Forces and promoters of British sport. They were making an effort to live as normal lives as possible without pulling rank; they had done nothing to deserve the persistent intrusion into their privacy to which the *News of the World* and its fellow scavengers had subjected them.

Inevitably and no doubt irritatingly for Harry, much had been made of his relationship with South African Chelsy Davy, who soon became a hot topic for the *News of the World*. The paper liked to speculate on her impatience with Harry's alleged shenanigans and in April 2006 splashed a story about it under the by-lines of royal editor Clive Goodman and Neville 'Onan the Barbarian' Thurlbeck.

Thurlbeck was the hard-nosed old hack who usually handled the muckier kiss-and-tell stories for whom a sting had gone badly wrong a few years earlier. He'd set out to expose a naturists' boarding house in Essex whose owners allegedly offered 'extra' sexual services to guests. Having made his investigations, Thurlbeck carelessly forgot to 'make his excuses and leave' (in the time-honoured *News of the World* manner). Instead, no doubt to his eternal regret, he was caught on film begging the couple to have sex while he stood at the foot of their bed, exposed what, in its primmer days, the News of the World would have called his 'manhood' and indulged in an unmistakable act of onanism. Since the film was posted on the internet to the delight of his fascinated colleagues, it was inevitable that sooner or later the moniker 'Onan the Barbarian', bestowed on him by an uncharitable ex-colleague, would stick.

The story Goodman and Thurlbeck had now worked on together was headlined:

FURY AFTER HE OGLED LAPDANCERS' BOOBS

Shame-faced Prince Harry has been given a furious Chelsy Davy dressing-down over his late night antics in a lapdancing bar. His loyal girlfriend discovered how strippers perched on the edge of his chair as he partied with a string of naked dancers and ogled their boobs. Yesterday the repentant Prince took an ear-bashing phone call as news broke.

"It's Chelsy. How could you? I see you had a lovely time without me. But I miss you so much, you big ginger, and I want you to know I love you," said a hysterical voice.

Luckily the caller was joker brother, Prince William. He thought the whole episode was hilarious and decided to take the mickey by putting on a high-pitched South African accent like Chelsy's.

What Goodman and Thurlbeck didn't reveal, although it's quite obvious with hindsight, was that this phone call was in fact a message left by Prince William on his brother's voicemail, and eavesdropped by Goodman.

Now, with Goodman accessing these private calls, it looked very much as if a serious crime had been committed – not just a slight digression from the Press Complaints Commission guidelines, but a clear-cut infringement of the Regulation of Investigatory Powers Act 2000 (RIPA), which makes it illegal for people to intercept communications in the course of transmission without the consent of the sender and recipient.

After the first rush of angry indignation at yet another callous violation of their privacy, in Clarence House, given all the deeply intrusive press activity which they had suffered over many years, the predominant reaction of the Royals and their staff was one of almost hopeless resignation. No one in the Royal circle was very surprised that someone had finally gone to these lengths, even less so given the newspaper involved. In the past, after all, private letters had been stolen and the most intimate conversations relayed across the world's media; it was almost inevitable that sooner or later someone would find a way of tapping into their private voicemails, if not directly into their conversations. As a result, special care had long been taken not to leave sensitive messages, yielding Goodman a very paltry crop of stories, from the hundreds of messages that he was later found to have intercepted. In any case, the Windsors had lived with such persistent intrusion over many years that they were to some extent inured to it as they stood back to watch the police investigation take its course.

CHAPTER TWO

A ROYAL RAT PACK

The news of the interceptions of the Clarence House mobile phones triggered alarms in several distant corners of Whitehall. There was a rumour that senior members of the government had been systematically 'bugged', along with a disparate group of politicians who, in view of what the papers liked to call their 'lifestyle', might be deemed to be vulnerable, or at least capable of yielding a story to excite the readers of the *News of the World*.

While the tabloids have always argued that politicians' private lives are fair game – in that many MPs will use the media to their own advantage as much as vice versa – there were real concerns that ministers' messages, some of a seriously secret nature, could have been lifted. It needed only a very small, one-off lapse of caution for a highly sensitive piece of information to be left on someone's voicemail. A senior officer in the anti-terrorist branch of the Metropolitan Police was detailed to run the investigation.

The principal tasks for the investigating officers were to scrutinise Clive Goodman's methods and establish what had motivated him to use them. As royal editor on the *News of the World*, Goodman's function was to supply a constant stream of news about the Royals. Inevitably there are periods in the life of any family, even the Windsors, when nothing much is going on, and it was tacitly accepted by editors that any snippets of gossip, however trivial, would do. If these snippets happened also to be stories which none of his rivals could produce, so much the better.

Thus, a steady run of small, intimate scooplets interspersed with the occasional meaty piece had kept him afloat for the past few years.

Now 48, Clive Goodman had been ploughing the royal furrow for nearly two decades and was one of the longest serving and most experienced of royal watchers. He'd originally learned the gossip trade during his six years on the *Daily Mail* diary page under Nigel Dempster, acknowledged king of tattle, whom Clive admired and aspired to emulate, although he knew he would never – could never – achieve the giddy influential heights of Dempster, who had married the daughter of a duke and was almost as grand as the aristos whose lives he chronicled. Clive, after all, had emerged from much humbler origin.

Clive Goodman was born on September 17, 1957 in the Hammersmith hospital. His mother, Margaret, took him home to the flat she occupied with her husband, Arthur, an accounts clerk with British Railways. Home was No.8, H-block, on the Peabody Housing Trust estate on Dalgarno Gardens in North Kensington, a complex of utilitarian, brick-built five-storey blocks of flats of no obvious aesthetic merit, though clean and benignly administered by the Trust.

After an unremarkable career at a West London school, in 1976 Clive joined the ranks of young trainee hacks who beaver away for a pittance in provincial newspapers while they learn the trade and study for their journalists' exams. Clive found himself a billet at the *Kentish Times*, a group of South London/North Kent papers and as good a place as any on which to cut his hack's teeth in pursuit of what he considered his natural destiny in Fleet Street. Clive is remembered at the Kent paper as an affable young man who got on well with his colleagues and was turning into a good, reliable reporter, handling all the usual stuff of local news as well as writing the record reviews.

Training with him was Deborah Lawrenson – now a best-selling novelist – with whom he became friends. When Clive was ready to fledge and flee the *Kentish Times*, he saw an opening on Nigel Dempster's page on the *Mail*. He applied and duly presented himself at New Carmelite House in Fleet Street. Dempster recognised useful qualities in the hungry 25 year-old and, despite the remnants of rough edges, took him on. Clive was ecstatic. It was exactly what he'd always dreamed of doing, and he was joining a famous and well-established team, where Adam Helliker, now gossip-in-chief at the Sunday Express, was 2 i/c.

Clive took to the job happily, showing an early aptitude for extracting information as he developed a cajoling, oleaginous manner that served him very well with greedy Palace footmen and playboy roués alike, opening doors for him at many levels. His wheedling, breathless tones – the result of a 4-pack-a-day cigarette habit – became well known to indiscreet people on the fringes of society and royal circles.

But he didn't forget Deborah and the next time an opening arose on the page, he phoned his chum at the *Kentish Times*. She came up, and also joined Dempster's then invincible team.

As a young reporter, Goodman was ambitious. He worked hard to fit in on the gossip page, disguising his North Ken housing estate origins and attempting to pass himself off as a man who might have come from a minor southern public school. He learned how to hold his knife and fork appropriately and developed a concise staccato English that almost disguised his social background – an undoubted requirement for the job. He wore big, bespoke double-breasted suits with overwide chalk stripes and slightly dodgy trimming which became part of his trade-mark persona – more well-to-do wine merchant than Fleet Street hack.

Goodman carved a name for himself at the *Mail*, sufficiently that in the late '80s he achieved promotion by being hired as royal correspondent at the *News of the World*. In many ways he was more at home in the Wapping newsroom and took the opportunity to raise his game. Having married in 1985, he was happy to settle down behind his desk and play the part of the royal tattler, with his iffy suits and old-fashioned 'gentlemanly' accessories, including a fob chain and even the occasional dangling monocle. With characteristic *News of the World* disregard for accuracy, his colleagues called him 'Raffles', after the fictitious, well-bred Victorian cracksman.

With hard work and the relentless milking of a growing list of contacts, a steady flow of titillating gossip and sporadic bursts of good, hard stories appeared beneath Goodman's keyboard-tapping fingers. His legendary if not very profound charm and a generous budget from his new managing editor enabled him to operate a wide range of information gatherers drawn from the Royal Households and from among the friends, acquaintances and assorted hangers-on to the Royal, rich or famous. He must sometimes have envied the ease with which some of his informers – people ostensibly with very little to bring to the party in terms of wealth, talent or beauty – could get so close to newsworthy personages simply by steadily worming their way into a particular circle until they became accepted members of it. Nevertheless Goodman lunched them, he flattered them, and above all, he paid them until it became the easiest way for them to make money, and they made sure they kept the stories coming.

In those earlier, glory days – when he'd been on top of every new twist in the disintegrating royal marriage and his by-line had appeared on the front page of the paper five weeks in a row – his deep coverage of the divorce, the Princess's affairs and her subsequent death had given him an impressive reputation. It was widely known, too, that at the high point of his career, the Princess had actually phoned to speak to him herself.

For the next ten years, though, he was under growing pressure to reproduce those high points, as different editors sought different strategies for making the best use of his still considerable, if declining talents. For a year or so, he'd been given a second-string column of his own, "The Carvery", which purported to reveal inappropriate behaviour and hypocrisy among the rich and famous.

In time, this vehicle ran out of steam or, at any rate, ceased to appear, but when in early 2006 the driving seat became vacant on Blackadder, an already established gossip column in the paper, Goodman was eased into it. This wasn't a promotion, more a matter of finding a slot for a once effective reporter who had lost his edge. But this didn't stop Goodman remaining deeply conscious of his position in the newsroom pecking order. Perhaps in the way the butler of a duke feels inevitably superior to that of a mere baronet, so he, who reported the Royals, was superior to those who reported the lives and misdemeanours of mere soap stars, WAGS and *Big Brother* contestants. It was a position that he cherished. But he was uncomfortably aware that it was fast slipping away.

At one point during this phase of his career, he lurched into a serious depression when he let a very major scoop slip through his fingers. Soon after he'd taken over the "Blackadder" column, a reliable freelance journalist had come to him with a strong, sensational tip-off: The Prince of Wales was to about to announce his engagement to Camilla Parker Bowles. Goodman, from what he considered his advantageous perspective, was sceptical. He rang Clarence House to check the story. When he put the phone down, he pronounced the story rubbish and on his strong advice, the editor spiked it.

Four days later, on February 10th, the story appeared in another paper. By 10am Clarence House had confirmed the story, and the world's media were running it. The following autumn, Goodman had still not fully recovered from the blow.

Goodman's editor, Andy Coulson, had been ambivalent, or at least obfuscating, in his approach to his royal editor's performance.

'I'm *sure* you're going to pull a good splash out of the bag for me soon,' he had quietly urged Goodman, ten years his senior, with an edge of irony in his clipped Estuary English. In fact he and Goodman were long-standing friends and it was probably only this that had kept Goodman where he was, long after his powers had so obviously dissipated. The truth was that by autumn '05, Goodman hadn't produced a good splash for some time. His last major scoop to really make the readers sit up had been the "HARRY'S DRUG SHAME" headline in January 2002, under which he shared a by-line with the paper's star investigator, Mazher Mahmood. They had worked many times together, as on the spectacular bust of James, Marquess of Blandford.

But Mazher had long since steamed ahead, keeping his own tight little team about him, and the papers biggest laurels had for some time been going to the Birmingham-born Pakistani with a genius for laying investigative traps. Meanwhile energetic, more inventive young thrusters like Brian Sabey were beginning to make their mark and overhaul Goodman in the pursuit of Royals. The pressure was getting to the royal editor. He'd divorced his first wife and recently remarried; he had a mortgage on a smart hacienda-style home in an exclusive Putney enclave and an 18-month-old daughter. He felt threatened and vulnerable. It was rumoured that he was no longer comfortable at the *News of the World*, scene of his greatest earlier triumphs, and was actively looking for a way out of the paper he'd worked on for almost twenty years.

Towards the end of 2005, Goodman's already wobbly self-esteem received a serious public knocking. Ian Edmondson, newly appointed Head of News, called his first weekly reporters meeting, the purpose of which was to set the agenda for the week and generally pep up the workers. Goodman hadn't turned up at a Tuesday morning meeting for years. He was, after all, royal editor, not a run-of-the-mill reporter. But Edmondson noticed his absence at that first meeting, and, either because he thought Goodman wasn't producing enough or had just got lazy, he decided to flex his authority by demanding that in future, Goodman must attend. Goodman's colleagues wondered whether or not Clive would show up the following week, and when he did, they were in no doubt about the humiliation he felt at being ordered to come.

The pressure to produce good splashes – bold shocking front pages that sell newspapers – was normal for any journalist working on a British national newspaper, more so on the popular 'Red Tops'. This was especially so on the Sunday titles, where writers had just one shot a week to make a splash, while their colleagues at the dailies had six. In addition, while journalists at the Sunday papers have longer to deliver a story, they have more time to lose it. A writer might walk into the office on a Tuesday with a brilliant idea, to which his editor says, 'Great! Go and do it.'

On Wednesday he'll go off to follow up on the story, setting up an interview for Thursday, leaving Friday to write it up. Then, Bosh! There's the Story, splashed all over a rival Saturday paper – a whole week's work up the spout, and just twelve hours left to produce something else to satisfy an ever-demanding editor.

These tensions inevitably lead to severe twitchiness in Sunday hacks.

And of the Sunday titles, the *News of the World*, in its time-honoured role as pre-eminent entertainer, scandalmonger and exposeur of "corruption", exerts the greatest pressure of all, particularly so at this point in Goodman's career, when newspaper readership generally had started to decline. Goodman knew as well as anyone on his paper that somehow, every week, he had to produce fresh stories that no one else could get near, and he'd planned long and hard in developing new ways to do it.

Other things also added to the pressure on Goodman. His new column had previously been the domain of former royal spin-doctor Mark Bolland, who was well known at Clarence House. The *Screws* claimed, with no substantiation, that the nickname "Lord Blackadder" (one of his politer aliases, it was said) had been coined for him by princes William and Harry, and then used to head his weekly gossip column. Bolland had not been happy to be replaced by Goodman. 'A dangerous man, is all I can say,' was how he would later describe his successor.

Although Goodman had at least as many good contacts as any royal reporter and strong ties with Palace domestic staff, the Princess's famous call notwithstanding, he'd never really had any special relationship with her, like those often (if speciously) claimed by his competitors. Since Diana had died, though, public interest had swung inevitably to her sons, and they were now the media's prime Royal Family targets.

This hadn't made Goodman's job easier. Physically it was becoming more difficult for him to pursue the stories in the way he once had. No longer a young man, he was under no illusion that he could usefully trawl Pangaea, Mamalanji, Boujis or Mahiki, the princes' preferred night spots, or infiltrate himself into weekend house parties or The Rattlebone Inn near Highgrove where Harry had practised his early bucolic boozing. Goodman had got into the habit of refusing to leave his office to follow the royal circus, preferring instead to stay at his desk and rely on his contacts to bring the stories to him. He became known among the other hacks of the Royal Rat Pack as the 'Eternal Flame' – because he never went out. They understood, too, that as a Sunday hack, he had to follow his own line and keep his own counsel.

Royal stories come under a category of their own in Fleet Street. Items that would be utterly trivial in anyone else's life take on great importance when attached to a central member of the Royal Family. From time to time there are non-royal subjects who appear to justify a similar degree of minute inspection by the British press – Liz

Hurley & Hugh Grant, David and Victoria Beckham, Pete Doherty or Amy Winehouse – but sooner or later all these people run out of currency and cease to captivate the public. The Royals, however, are always with us, and the public appetite for details of their lives never dries, for they are, of course, the supreme reality soap opera.

In an era which has seen the extraordinary rise of magazines based only on celebrity gossip – *Hello!*, *OK*, *Heat* – the old-school royal reporters always considered themselves a cut above the rest of the hacks. Men like Harry Arnold for *The Sun* and James Whitaker for the *Mirror*, who led the Royal Rat Pack since the 1970s, became great experts in the minutiae of the Royals' lives.

The BBC has also had its dedicated royal correspondents, but these tended to be more conventional, and as representatives of the national broadcaster, snooping wasn't part of their brief. Jenny Bond and, more recently, Nicholas Witchell prided themselves on having formal, internal lines of communication with Buckingham Palace, but Princess Diana and her particular way of interacting with the press generated an explosion of interest that had changed much about reporting on the Royals. While James Whitaker liked to put across the idea that he had a personal relationship with the Princess, it was, in fact another royal reporter, Richard Kay of the *Daily Mail*, with whom she preferred to speak.

Characteristic of royal reporters is the curious symbiosis in which they live with their targets. It matters to some of them, especially the more traditional, even respectful among them, that they feel they have a special rapport with one or other member of the Royal Family. They pride themselves on an intimate knowledge of the minutest detail of the family and its accoutrements. Any little bit of tittle-tattle is a potential front-page story. A thorough knowledge was a great bonus to seasoned professionals like Harry Arnold and James Whitaker.

For instance, when Princess Diana was still alive, they could home in on a piece of jewellery she was wearing and extract some significance from it. Who had given it to her? Was it Prince Charles? Why was she wearing it after her divorce? Could that mean they were getting back together? If Diana revisited a holiday resort where she'd been with Prince Charles before their divorce, the connection would be made, and the trip would be described as 'a painful stroll down memory lane' for the Princess.

Whitaker, who was especially adept at making these and more arcane links, was considered by most to be the doyen of the Royal Rat Pack. Educated at Cheltenham College, James Whitaker had started his career proper, like Clive Goodman, on the *Daily Mail* diary. Assigned one of his first royal stories, he'd gone to cover a polo match in which Prince Charles was playing and was served smoked salmon and champagne.

'I decided from that day on royal reporting was the most civilised job in journalism,' he has said of his career.

Whitaker made his name after that on the *Daily Star* and ultimately ended up on the *Mirror* on an enviable salary. He was known by a few other monikers – 'Widow Twanky' for his pantomime dameishness, or 'the Big Red Tomato'. Bulky and full-bellied, Whitaker enjoyed the high-life that went with the job and extended it into his private life. If asked to shoot grouse, he would heave out his 12-bores and head North without a moment's hesitation, and he loved a day at the races, passing on this enthusiasm to his eldest son Edward, now chief photographer for the *Racing Post*. Whitaker's nose for sniffing out fine restaurants wherever he was in the world was legendary.

His stories were filled with breathless self-importance – 'I can exclusively reveal,' his opening would gush, usually to be rewritten by *Mirror* subs as, 'The Mirror can exclusively reveal.' In truth his royal contacts were little better than anyone else's, but that didn't stop him promoting the myth of his intimate sources with such self-assurance and gusto that TV crews from around the world would flock to the *Mirror* offices to quiz him about the latest royal crisis.

'Don't brief me beforehand on the questions,' he would bellow at them. 'Just fire away.' He never turned down a chance to appear on TV, and both his profile as the royal hack most-in-the-know and his income burgeoned.

'I do nothing for free, you should know that by now,' he would tell terrified TV researchers who rang to ask him to appear.

Harry Arnold, his best-known rival since before Charles and Diana were even an item, was small and dapper. Quick-witted and always immaculately turned out, Arnold was always fun to have around, a wonderful raconteur and popular in the Royal Rat Pack, of which he and Whittaker were founding members. Born and brought up in Kent, Arnold secured more scoops on Princess Diana and Prince Charles than any other royal reporter and was responsible for fulfilling editor Kelvin MacKenzie's royal agenda, though, mischievously Kelvin loved to catch Arnold out.

Some days he would swing into *The Sun* newsroom screaming, 'Arnold you 'orrible little man. What is Prince Charles having for breakfast?'

If Arnold didn't know, he'd be mock-bollocked in front of all.

Arnold claimed to have had a contact so close to Prince Charles that he knew what the Prince said to Diana on the balcony of Buckingham Palace after their wedding in 1981.

'Kiss me,' Diana had pleaded.

'I'm not getting into that caper,' he'd replied, before acquiescing.

In the face of much scepticism from his rivals, a lip-reader subsequently confirmed these exact words from a video of the event.

Eventually Arnold grew tired of being booted around the newsroom by Kelvin MacKenzie and left *The Sun* in the early '90s to become chief reporter at the *Mirror*.

Perhaps Arnold's closest rival in breaking big stories was the urbane *Daily Mail* man, Richard Kay. As well as having a direct line to Princess Diana, Kay's sources were always impeccable. Now the paper's diarist, having taken over from Nigel Dempster, Kay shows a rare knack for persuading important people to talk to him, with the benefit of being immensely charming and liked by everyone. A painstaking journalist, when he worked the royal beat during the early '90s, he was untouchable and the rest of the pack grew weary of having to pursue his agenda-setting scoops week after week.

Among the flock of photographers that swarms around the Royal Family with a distressing lack of dignity is Arthur Edwards, who worked with Arnold on *The Sun*. Cockney Edwards, who's still at it, has always thought a lot of himself and is billed by *The Sun* as the man 'who knew the Royals best', always bantering with them on Royal tours. 'Arfur' even brought out a book of photos of Princess Diana with the title *I'll Tell The Jokes, Arthur*, which she'd once famously quipped when he was getting a little above himself.

Photographer Kent Gavin worked with Whitaker on the *Mirror*. An Essex-born Arsenal supporter, he was the most respected amongst the Royal Rat Pack for always keeping his head. If a Royal's detective ever needed to reprimand photographers for getting too close to Diana (which was frequently), Gavvers was always the one who'd represent the group and negotiate. Although not averse to a drink, Gavin was a brilliant photographer and had won a hoard of awards for the *Mirror* before he became a full-time royal snapper. In fact his bosses thought so much of him it was written into his contract that he was entitled to travel Club Class everywhere – a rare privilege for a staff snapper.

It was to this intimate cosy little band that Clive Goodman might have done well to cleave himself, although when it came to it, he never felt enormously comfortable as part of the pack. Besides, it was quite early in his royal watching days that he had started to rely on the stories coming to him, rather than going out to find them.

If there was a clear distinction between royal correspondents and the hoi polloi hacks, there was an even more marked distinction between the journalistic style of those who worked on what used to be called the broadsheets (*The Times, Telegraph, Guardian*) and those on the 'Red Tops' (the *Mirror, The Sun*, the *Star* and the *Screws*).

There is a long-standing myth in Fleet Street that writers on tabloids are generally better at the job than their broadsheet counterparts. The received idea is that it's harder to tell a story or explain a complex piece of news in short, pithy sentences than in the expansive style of a quality hack. I am not a journalist and have never felt any peer pressure to swallow this improbable notion, though I've heard many good journalists subscribe to the concept, perhaps out of good old-fashioned English middle-class modesty.

There is, nevertheless, undoubtedly a more robust tradition of camaraderie, shared risk-taking and neck-stretching among the tabloid reporters. In the days when Fleet Street was still Fleet Street, the 'Red Top' hacks would gather most evenings with the 'serious' scribes from the quality press in El Vino's and the other watering-holes along the famous road and swap tales of scoop-gathering and derring-do. As the presses clattered away behind them, spewing out the first editions, it was safe to come clean and admit to your rivals what story you'd been working on that day.

With the flow of booze, so the flow of well-worn tales would burgeon, old wrinkled stories of how the great scoops were won. The tabloid hacks always had the best tales of cleverness and resourcefulness. They'd had to seek out the murky places where their kind of stories happened, while the serious writers mouldered in their office writing about Government Foreign Policy. Exposing a footballer's illicit leg-over was, in tabloid hacks' view, a far better way to spend your working day than trying to explain an arcane Act of Parliament.

All nonsense, of course, but it was always entertaining to hear the smart-arse tricks and cons a tabloid hack had used to stand his story up – like the reporter who'd been tipped off about a soap star playing away with a 'glamorous blonde'.

It so happened that this particular reporter knew only the name of the lover and where she worked, and he badly needed a photo. He grabbed his photographer and off they raced to a business park on the outskirts of a sprawling town in the south of England, where she worked in a large office. He wanted an interview if possible, or at least a picture, which was crucial for a tabloid story.

When he and his snapper arrived outside the large concrete and glass building, it became clear that it would be harder than he'd anticipated to identify the woman from among the 500 or so people who worked there. In addition, the hack had no idea what the woman in question looked like (apart from being blonde and 'attractive', which was too subjective to be helpful). He couldn't ring her on the phone and request an interview because she'd undoubtedly give him the brush off, realise the press were on to her and seek escape via a back exit. Nor could he raise suspicions by asking every blonde coming out for lunch whether she was the right woman.

Thinking with tabloid alacrity, he rang a local florist and ordered the biggest bunch of white lilies they had and sent them anonymously to her in the office. Confident that his plans were laid, he went off for a long lunch before returning to the photographer's car later in the afternoon, when he sat back and waited.

At 5.00pm, people started streaming from the building. The

hack and the snapper discretely scrutinised the passing throng until 5.30pm, when a woman clutching a bunch of white lilies emerged from the building and strode off to the car park. She was blonde, and both men agreed that she was attractive. The photographer sat bolt upright and triggered his motor-drive to get a set of pictures through the windscreen of the car. But the reporter had to be sure they were the lilies he'd sent. He leaped from the car, bounded up to her, asked her name and requested an interview. She turned him down flat, but only after she'd confirmed who she was. The tabloid team had a sensational set of pictures and a definite name, which would guarantee them the splash in the next day's paper.

Later that evening, as they toasted their success, the photographer asked the hack why he'd sent such a large bunch of lilies. 'Simple,' he replied. 'If the bunch was small, she'd have kept them in the office and never walked out with them. I guessed if the bunch was big enough, she'd take at least half home and leave the rest in the office to cheer her up tomorrow. Any woman would rather have lilies at home than in the office.'

That's the way a tabloid writer's mind works – clever and creative. And if this reporter's actions were highly intrusive and not to everyone's taste, his methods were worthy nevertheless of a little sneaking admiration. They were also entirely legal, unlike those Clive Goodman ultimately chose to acquire his stories.

CHAPTER THREE

A SCOOP AT ANY PRICE

Tuesday, August 8, 2006

On the second Tuesday in August, 2006, in a well-worn, bow-fronted semi in a South London suburb, Glenn Mulcaire's eyes flickered open and registered the dawn light seeping through the curtains drawn across the bedroom window. He knew it was too early and rolled over to glance at the clock beside the bed.

He winced. It was 6.00am.

He hadn't planned to get up for another hour. He wondered what had disturbed him and glanced at his wife, Alison, beside him, with her auburn hair splayed out across the pillow. Whatever had disturbed him had passed her by and she was still sleeping deeply, as she always did after long days of caring for their five active children. Glenn was glad she was getting her sleep but he thought he might as well start his own day now. He had a lot of work on – urgent inquiries to follow up for News International, his sole, demanding client. He had wanted to do these jobs the previous evening, but he'd been sidetracked into discussing future projects at AFC Wimbledon, the fledgling community football club he'd helped to found five years before. Decisively, he thought if he got up now and drove over to his small office premises, where all of his IT equipment and records were stored, he could knock the jobs on the head and see what else had come in.

He swung his legs over the side of the bed and, emerging fully from his sleep, he identified the sound that had woken him as the throb of a single-engined chopper, now evidently swinging round and heading back towards his home. He wondered why the hell a helicopter was cruising low over the roofs of Cheam at this hour on a Saturday morning, especially when it seemed now to be directly overhead, and not moving on. Thinking he might be able to see it from the bedroom window, he walked over to twitch a curtain aside.

Before he had a chance to look up at the sky, the scene in the tree-lined, car-filled street outside instantly absorbed all his attention and filled him with dread. Two police cars were parked in the road directly outside his house, with two more at each end, blocking both exits to the short scruffy avenue. The chopper above grew louder while it gently eased itself over the house and came into view, with the word 'POLICE' starkly visible on the underside as it began once more to hover.

Glenn felt as if his innards had been grabbed by a giant hand and were being slowly twisted. Physically fit and conversant with his body's reactions, he felt his heart rate quicken as adrenaline flooded into his system. He knew the police were there for him. Although the possibility had lurked in the back of his mind for over a year, he'd always successfully pushed it aside so it wouldn't interfere with his work. He'd tell himself he was being a tad paranoid; that what he was doing, while touching the limits, was still OK.

Of course, from time to time he'd had ethical, even moral problems with his methods, but they fell plausibly within the remit of the technical research services he was under contract to supply to News International, principally to the *News of the World*. Now, in a flash of enlightenment, he knew his actions had been wrong. The police outside his house – who any moment would wake his wife and children and everyone else in the street, no doubt – confirmed unequivocally what his conscience had been whispering ever since he'd begun intercepting people's private communications.

He'd been wrong to do it; he knew it, and now he was going to pay for it. Extraordinarily, in a matter of a few moments, the next emotion to course through him was a profound sense of relief: it was all over. Mulcaire took a deep breath, composed himself and walked downstairs just as the first policeman left his car. By the time he opened the front door, a small crowd had gathered in the small patch of front garden between Glenn's gleaming 4x4 and Alison's smaller family car. Three plain-clothes men barged into the house before he had a chance to invite them. Following close behind came another, waving a piece of paper and holding his badge up for inspection.

'Glenn Mulcaire, we have a warrant for your arrest under anti-terrorist powers and the RIPA Act, 2002....' – which he pronounced as 'ripper' – 'and we have a warrant to search your house. Anything you say may be recorded and used in evidence against you.'

Glenn heard the baby crying and the rest the family beginning to stir upstairs, while he regulated his breath and prepared himself to assure them that there was nothing to worry about. Nothing to worry about? he thought. But he kept calm, even scrutinising the warrant that had been thrust under his nose, while he acknowledged to himself the absolute inevitability of what was happening.

While the police and their extensive back-up surrounded Glenn Mulcaire's house in Cheam, about six miles due north another group from the anti-terrorist squad arrived in the quiet, exclusive cul-de-sac on Putney's West Hill where Goodman lived with his wife and young daughter. This group also had an arrest warrant. Goodman was driven to Charing Cross Police Station, where he was charged and released through the front in a blaze of camera flash, while Mulcaire was questioned at Belgravia Police Station, where he was charged under anti-terrorist laws. Two days later Mulcaire would be released without a press camera in sight.

Later on the day of the arrests, the police released details of their actions and Fleet Street was suddenly the epicentre of seismic shock-waves as the story flashed round the globe, causing tremors in newsrooms everywhere.

At 9.24pm BST, a report was filed by the international news agency the Associated Press:

British police arrest 3 suspects after phone-tapping complaint from Prince Charles.
BYLINE: Beth Gardiner, AP Writer

British police arrested three men including a newspaper section editor Tuesday in an investigation that began with complaints from Prince Charles' office about possible phone-tapping, police and the paper said.

Police said they did not believe the phones of any members of the Royal Family had been tapped. But other public figures may have had their calls intercepted, raising potential security issues, the police said. They refused to specify who.

Police did not identify those who were arrested but the *News of the World* tabloid said Clive Goodman, editor of its section on royalty, was among them.

Hayley Barlow, a spokesman for the Sunday newspaper, declined to comment further.

The investigation was prompted by complaints from Charles' Clarence House office to the police's royalty protection department.

"It is focused on alleged repeated security breaches within telephone networks over a significant period of time and the potential impact this may have on protective security around a number of individuals," London's Metropolitan Police said in a statement.

Charles' office declined to comment on the arrests.

Police said they had arrested three men, ages 35, 48 and 50. All were arrested at their homes in London under the Regulation of Investigatory Powers Act.

Police said they had searched two of the residences, along with business addresses in the Wapping, Sutton and Chelsea neighbourhoods.

Anti-terrorism officers are leading the investigation and police are working with phone companies in an effort to identify all those whose conversations were tapped, they said.

The story had also been picked up and transmitted by other major agencies, The Press Association and Agence France Presse. CNN's London bureau relayed the story with a transatlantic slant reflecting Murdoch's position in the US media. It appeared in the late editions of all the British national and major regional dailies, in some cases with more than a whiff of *schadenfreude*.

News of the world?

Roy Greenslade – former editor of the *Daily Mirror*, now media commentator and premier scourge of the tabloids – wrote about it in the London *Evening Standard* and made much of the irony that the *News of the World* had been caught with its pants firmly round its ankles, running exactly the kind of scam it loved to report. He went on to remind readers of a series of court decisions against the paper and bungles perpetrated by it under Andy Coulson over the past few months, describing it as a "rogue paper that continually tests the limits of a code of practice specifically drawn up by editors to curb bad behaviour."

On the other side of the Atlantic, the story made the early editions of *The Seattle Post-Intelligencer, The Windsor Star, Ontario, The New York Times* as well as the 7.00am news on *NBC*, and in Australia, *The Sydney MX* afternoon paper, until it was picked up by hundreds of papers, wire services, radio and television stations across the world. Rupert Murdoch's News Corp was the proprietor of newspapers in four continents; there was bound to be interest in events at his largest selling title, and the world's best-selling Sunday paper.

***

When Rupert Murdoch bought the paper in 1969, the *News of the World* was already over 125 years old.

Our motto is the truth; our practice is the fearless advocacy of the truth.

With these fine sentiments, the *News of the World* was launched on October 1, 1843 by John Browne Bell, with a cover price of 3d. In its earliest incarnations, the paper set out worthily to provide a clear, concise and objective summary of the week's news for manual workers and tradesmen who didn't read the daily papers. Published in several consecutive editions between Friday and Sunday morning, it was described by the *Newspaper Press Directory* of 1847:

> Ultra-liberal. This is one of the many papers that compress into a capacious double-sheet the news of the week. And the manner in which it is arranged adapts it for the perusal of a class of reader

who, though respectable, may be supposed – through incessant occupation during the week – not to have had much opportunity before the Saturday evening for newspaper reading. It has no very distinctive feature in its composition, which simply aims at giving as much news as possible, of a general as well as a particular character. There is some attention given to literature, and a small selection of sporting news. Its commercial intelligence is good and its "Grocers' Gazette" seems to mark it out as favoured by that class of traders. It is well suited to respectable tradesmen and intelligent persons in that sphere and its cheapness tends, of course, to enlarge the circle of its readers. It appears to be designed in a great degree for country circulation and the main feature of its management is the number of its editions – in fact Friday evening to Sunday morning there is a perpetual succession of editions with augmented if not emended intelligence so as to secure for every post through which it is sent out the latest news from every source.

After a fairly successful launch (albeit with sales that look minuscule by today's standards), the paper lurched uncertainly towards the end of the century. When in 1890 the oppressive stamp duty that had been levied by successive governments was finally abolished, the Bells were, unlike their competitors, slow to drop the cover price and as a result sales languished. The paper sickened, and by 1891, the Bells were in trouble and sold the paper to Lascelles Carr, already the owner of a successful paper in Cardiff, the *Western Mail*. His first editor was his nephew, Emsley Carr, who occupied the seat for the next 50 years. At the same time, Lascelles Carr's lawyer, George Riddell, effectively took over the direction of the paper.

Over the next half century, Riddell introduced all sorts of sales promotions and cash prize competitions while expanding into the hitherto undersupplied Scottish Sunday market. Emsley Carr established the main editorial thrust of the paper, headlining on sexual shenanigans and general misbehaviour – preferably of the rich and famous, or, failing that, of anyone who ought to have known better, or not. This tendency toward prurience disguised as morality had deep roots in the culture of the British popular Sunday press, as characterised in 1785 by the commentator George Crabbe, following the launch of *The Sunday Monitor*, with its disingenuous exterior...

Then lo, the sainted Monitor is born,
Whose pious face some scared texts adorn
As artful sinners cloak the secret sin,
To veil with seeming grace the guile within
So moral essays on his front appear
But all is carnal business in the rear.

In the years following the Great War, the *News of the World* more or less abandoned even the pretence of "moral essays," which remained only as short, bland pep-talks, and the "carnal business" was promoted from the rear to the front page. Nevertheless, despite a seemingly infinite supply of lurid tales of human failing, the paper still insisted it was a "family" paper with an identifiable moral purpose and retained for many decades well past the next World War the use of mealy-mouthed euphemistic code words to describe rape and other sexual misdemeanour – clothes were "disarranged", ladies were "molested". Even today the language of the News of the World is a little more weasely and purse-lipped than that of her bonking-mad daily sister, *The Sun*.

So successful were Riddell and Emsley that by the time Emsley died in 1941, he had seen the circulation rise from 40,000 to 4.4 million. Ten years later his successors, Percy Davies and Robert Skelton, had boosted that to 8.4 million per week, making it by far the dominant popular newspaper in Britain, and, indeed, the most successful in the free world.

As the '50s unfolded and the British crept from under a blanket of wartime austerity, a little more glamour seeped into the pages of the News of the World, along with the daily tabloids, with stories of stars such as Brigitte Bardot and Diana Dors, as well as mink-&-yacht folk, Sir Bernard and Lady Docker. But nothing could have prepared readers for the scandal to end all scandals that broke in the early '60s, a tabloid blow-out boasting every possible salacious ingredient (except, admittedly, a clergyman). The story of Christine Keeler and Cabinet Minister John Profumo fed Fleet Street's smut-lust for many ecstatic months and beyond, loosening many of the traditional constraints in time for the sexual free-for-all to follow in the latter half of the '60s. Anyone was fair game if he had a skeleton in his cupboard. And, with the bar now raised so high on public shockability, the muck-raking had to be intensified and handled ever more creatively.

At the same time, in the 20 years since the war, television had become both a major competitor for the public's leisure time and a reliable source of personalities whose sexual adventures (and misadventures) could be vicariously enjoyed by *News of the World* readers. Nevertheless, the net effect of increased TV viewing was that sales of all newspapers, having been broadly static across the board, began slowly to decline. The *News of the World*, though affected, still reigned supreme – at least, in terms of sales, but not, it emerged in the late '60s, in profitability.

The *Screws* was by then a great flabby beast of an organisation, with a management far too immersed in its existing culture to see what needed to be done, and profits *pro rata* turnover were negligible. It was still largely owned and headed up by Sir William Carr, son of Emsley Carr. Sir William, it was widely noted, liked a drink. He was indeed seldom sober after midday and was popularly known as Pissy Billy. His hand on the tiller was not steady, and in 1968, his cousin, Professor Derek Jackson, who also held a large chunk of equity, announced that he wanted to sell his shares. Pissy Billy didn't have the money to buy them, and, as rumours spread, their price rose until they were acquired by Robert Maxwell, who proceeded to mount a substantial bid for the rest of the company.

Carr's editor at the time was Stafford Somerfield, who'd taken the chair in 1959, and broadly been allowed to get on with it by his proprietor. At Carr's urging, he willingly wrote a vitriolic and frankly xenophobic front-page article, decrying the aims of the thoroughly un-British "Jan Ludwig Hoch", Robert Maxwell's birth name. He said that the *News of the World* was 'as English as roast beef and Yorkshire pudding', and pointed out that not only was Maxwell a foreigner, he was also a Labour MP and would deprive the paper of its independence.

Against this promising backdrop, the little-known 37-year-old

Rupert Murdoch flew into London from Australia. Murdoch was the son of Sir Keith Murdoch, a respected Australian war correspondent and newspaper owner. Sir Keith died in 1952 while Rupert, after Geelong Grammar School, was in England reading Philosophy, Politics and Economics at Worcester College, Oxford. Sir Keith had expressed in his Will that if his son was considered 'worthy of support', he should join the *Adelaide News* as a journalist. After a short stint as a subeditor at the *Daily Express* in London, Rupert returned to Australia to become managing director of the respectable, if not especially profitable Adelaide newspaper company, News Ltd.

With a clear hint of what was to come, he focused on scandal, show business gossip and sport. Sales rocketed. With the surge in profits, he was able to buy major papers in Sydney and Perth and launch Australia's first and most successful television magazine, *TV Week*.

In 1964, at the age of 33, Murdoch boldly launched the first national daily newspaper in the country, a broadsheet called *The Australian*. He had shrewdly recognised a gap in the market in the increasingly independent and self-confident nation, at the same time securing for himself a significant level of gravitas and political influence. Once *The Australian* had consolidated into a successful and profitable paper, Murdoch was in a position to spread his wings and look for a foothold in the bigger and more influential milieu of the British press.

Towards the end of 1968, Sir William Carr was anxiously casting about for ways to block the approaches of the overbearing and unsubtle Robert Maxwell. In what turned out to be a fatal act of desperation, he contacted Rupert Murdoch and invited him to London, with a view to negotiating a merger in which the Carrs would at least retain control over the paper that had been in their family for over 75 years. Murdoch had read Somerfield's tirade against Maxwell, which he guessed must have been published at Carr's urging, and recognised the fear behind Carr's invitation. He arrived in London confident in the knowledge that he would have the upper hand in negotiations.

Having fed and charmed two other members of the Carr family at the Mirabelle, Murdoch arrived early in the morning at Sir William

Carr's house, since 'Pissy Billy' was generally too drunk to do business after 10.30am. Carr's banker, Harry Sporborg, was waiting with Carr. Murdoch opened the batting with his habitual frankness, saying that unless it was agreed from the outset that he would have full executive control of the paper and the company which published it, there would be no more discussion.

Sir William was aghast, spluttered that he couldn't accede to that and started rambling on about ways of keeping control in the family.

After listening for a short while, Murdoch, who must have been very sure of his ground and, in any case, was always a gambler, reiterated his fundamental condition, adding, 'I've come at my expense. It has cost you nothing. I'll cut my losses and go home if we can't agree right now.'

Sir William looked apoplectic and said nothing. Murdoch gave them a moment or two before nodding, 'G'day' and getting up to leave. Before he got to the door, Harry Sporborg pleaded to his departing back that he and Sir William should have five minutes in which to discuss Murdoch's suggestion. Murdoch agreed, and asked if he could wait in a room with a phone. While there he rang the Australian Prime Minister and asked if he could export several million Australian dollars at short notice. When he walked back in to see Sir William, his conditions had been agreed.

Murdoch mortgaged his entire Australian business to do the deal, and on January 5, 1969, it was announced that the shareholders of the *News of the World* had reached an agreement with News Ltd of Australia. Murdoch had taken his first step in what was to become his domination of the world's press. It was announced, too, that Sir William Carr would stay on in the figurehead position of chairman, but although he'd no inkling at the time, that was the beginning of the end for him. Within months he was pushed out of his chairmanship, and within the year, Murdoch also said goodbye to editor, Stafford Somerfield.

At the same time, Murdoch was also buying *The Sun* from Hugh Cudlipp of IPC, once again from under the nose of Robert Maxwell. This was an obvious move for Murdoch, not least because it would use up the huge spare printing capacity at the *News of the World*'s tatty old premises in Bouverie Street. Murdoch was helped in buying

The Sun for next to nothing by assiduously courting, with promises and blandishments, the print union leader, Richard Briginshaw. (Briginshaw must have indeed smarted 16 years later when Murdoch neutered the formerly rampant unions with his move to the revolutionary new print works at Wapping, with the loss of 5,000 print union jobs.)

Murdoch had a clear view of how he intended to run the *News of the World* and appointed a series of mostly like-minded editors to implement his vision. The first decade or so saw few major changes to the general tone of the paper, just more of the same – but nastier. When *Private Eye* dubbed Murdoch the '*Dirty Digger*', the name stuck.

Typical, and one of the more entertaining *News of the World* exposés of the early '70s, was the story of Under Secretary of State at the Ministry of Defence, Lord Lambton, who was caught smoking cannabis in bed with two prostitutes. The story was illustrated with a photograph taken by the husband of one of the women, Norma Levy. He was also caught on cine film, and an audio recording of proceedings was obtained using a microphone hidden in the nose of a Teddy bear perched handily beside the bed. It turned out that the girls worked for a madame whose clients included the then Leader of the House of Lords, Earl Jellicoe, who, like Lambton, had to resign his post.

In the course of an interview with MI5 officers regarding a possible breach of MoD security, Lambton explained that he had resorted to a combination of 'vigorous gardening' and 'debauchery' as a means of dealing with stress and the 'futility' of his job. It's fair to say that afterwards he didn't give the impression that his life had been ruined by the revelations. He admitted to having been serially unfaithful to his wife, and indeed, with unusual candour, told Robin Day in a subsequent interview, 'People sometimes like variety. I think it's as simple as that, and I think that impulse is probably understood by almost everybody. Don't you?'

Over the first 25 years of Murdoch's ownership, the News of the World was edited in a more or less traditional manner by a number of able and well-respected newspapermen – Bernard Shrimsley, Derek Jameson and David Montgomery among them – but Murdoch took a significant change of direction in the mid '90s. After the six-year reign of the reliable if not outstanding Patsy Chapman (who had succeeded another tough woman, Wendy Henry), Murdoch was looking for a new breed of editor and having recognised the growing market for gossip – as delivered by *Heat* and *OK* – he was ready to make a radical choice.

The *News of the World*'s sister daily, *The Sun*, was currently being edited by the famously energetic, inspired and foul-mannered Kelvin Mackenzie, and under his tutelage had burgeoned a bright, effective young reporter whom Kelvin had appointed to run *The Sun*'s show business page, *Bizarre*, then as now considered an important element of the paper.

Piers Morgan had never been ashamed of his ambition and did not suffer noticeably from false modesty, but even he was shocked by Murdoch's decision to appoint him editor of the country's biggest selling paper at the tender age of 28. The appointment of a young, ex-*Bizarre* journalist to edit the News of the World was a strong reflection of the growing demand for gossip and TV-trivia-led stories and set a precedent for the new emphasis of the paper. Hard news was pushed even further to the bottom of the agenda, and all effort was focused on mean-spirited stories with celebrity names attached – and the bigger they were, the harder they fell.

The *Screws*, along with the rest of the bottom-feeding media, liked to build up a new celebrity, sometimes on the flimsiest foundations – a large pair of breasts, say, or a personal weakness with which readers might be expected to empathise, or feel relieved they didn't possess. Because the journalists believe they have "created" the celebrities in the first place, they choose when and how to destroy them – ashes to ashes – with a clear conscience. In this distorted arrangement, the TV companies work symbiotically with the tabloids by producing shows such as *Big Brother* and its mutations, and facilitating access to their 'stars'. Reality TV shows now provide the perfect breeding ground for instant, spurious celebrity which is easily manipulated. Even if the TV companies do honour the public vote (and who monitors their polls?), they can always manufacture the result they want by the cynical editing of the 24/7 coverage. The resulting savaged victims have been many and various, suffering more acutely, no doubt, through having their tenuous sojourn at the celebrity trough cut short – dim Chantelle, twitching Pete or bonking Ziggy – to be paraded by the tabloids like Christians in the Roman Coliseum, teased and devoured for the diversion of the masses.

As well as the footballers' WAGs and *Big Brother* wannabes, the much-targeted Royal Family has also arrived at celebrity with no particular qualification – other than parentage. Unlike them, however, the Royal Family's fame was not facilitated by the junk media, but they and their associates have always been (and much more so in the last two decades) the subject of incessant press intrusion. And, like the pop culture mini-stars, they too are more or less defenceless to the whims of the media.

Built up, adored. Brought down, despised.

The lives of the British Royal Family are shamelessly scrutinized throughout the world – dissected and picked over by the media to a point where only their innermost feelings remain private, and even those are subject to perpetual speculation by a horde of royal hacks employed to surmise, fantasise and pronounce on them. The *News of the World*, the property of a self-proclaimed republican, is the undoubted leader of the scavenger pack – and it is determined to remain leader.

Since Murdoch bought the paper, the public's appetite for deeply intrusive royal and celebrity news has been cultivated and sustained vigorously through a series of editors. And since the late '80s, behind glamour-puss editors like Piers Morgan and Rebekah Wade, has stood an eminence gris, largely unknown to the public, the quiet but potent legal boss of News International, Tom Crone. Crone, regarded as the sharpest brief in the newspaper industry, wields the ultimate power of veto over what goes into the Murdoch tabloids. It is Crone who can assess better than anyone the risk/reward in running a calumnious celebrity story. At least eight editors have come and gone under Crone's 20-year watch, and in that time there has been a substantial toll of personal misery, damage and fear engendered by the papers.

A former *News of the World* journalist describes it thus....

'What you have to imagine is that in the hell's kitchen that is the News of the World newsroom, where a horde of little devils rake muck, lie, invent anything they think will titillate and tempt a less than diligent public into hating, sneering at or despising someone else, preferably someone they once admired because they were in *Corrie* or played for Man U or won *Big Brother*, or used to be married to a prince, and sometimes just unfortunate members of the public who were in the wrong place.... there, behind a string of editors, stands Crone, the legal ringmeister always on hand to tell them just how far they can go, and what it will cost them if they do transgress, so they can balance that against additional sales.'

Crone's fearsome reputation has been built on the many occasions he's proved he can stay within the law while walking the knife edge between fact and fantasy. Evidently, given the multitude of successful libel suits brought against the paper, either he doesn't always get it right or headstrong editors have failed to heed his advice. Crone is confident of a permanent billet in his sphere, as Kelvin Mackenzie revealed in a piece about the cost of libel at News International. Interviewed while making a TV programme on the subject, Crone suggested that he would never be unemployed as a libel lawyer for three reasons:

"Sometimes journalists deliberately mislead people.
Sometimes journalists get it plain wrong.
Sometimes people lie, and keep on lying for financial or image reasons. Archer and Aitken have been caught. Others have got away with it, and others will try it on in the future."

Piers Morgan, although a self-confessed royalist and besotted fan of Princess Diana, didn't stint in urging his royal editor Clive Goodman to do and spend whatever it took to cover the pantomime that the Princess's sex-life had become, with all the fringe players around it. Goodman delivered suitable remuneration and the customary lunch (often with news exec Bob Warren) at Langan's to any of his phalanx of contacts, and he was pulling in story after story. Famously, one of Goodman's minor royal stories very nearly backfired badly, but the manner in which Morgan handled it demonstrated the amazing capacity of agile tabloid minds to rescue triumph from adversity.

Piers breathlessly recounts the event in his book, *The Insider*. Earl Spencer, for some time not on the best of terms with Victoria, his wife and mother of his four children, was sick of stories about their marriage being leaked to the tabloids by people who posed as his good friends. He strongly suspected one of them of selling stories about his marriage to the *News of the World* and decided to deal with him and the paper at the same time. He wrote a letter to the supposed leaker...

> Victoria is in a clinic called Farm Place in Surrey, she needs all her old friends around her now. Please don't tell her I encouraged you to get in touch – it's better if she thinks you did it just because you loved her. I'm off to work for an American TV station in New York for a couple of years. I'll be taking the children too, but making sure that Victoria has frequent access. I think she might consider a move to the States herself, a couple of years away from Britain will be good for us all. Take care and I'll see you before I'm off, hopefully. Charles.

Piers must have jumped up and down with glee when Goodman produced a copy of the letter. He ran a front-page splash on it, along with a scathing leader, telling the Earl how callous and heartless he was to treat his sick wife so. They put in a call for comment to Spencer's office at 6.00pm, as the first edition was being put to bed. However, there was no response until 9.00pm, when the presses had already been rolling for an hour and a half.

'Mr Morgan, this is Earl Spencer. I've got you now, you bastard!' Spencer declared that he'd deliberately sent the letter to the paper's source, knowing that the recipient wouldn't be able to resist passing it on for the *News of the World* to publish. And it was all rubbish! He cackled manically. 'Now you're going to have to admit you've printed lies, aren't you, and apologise.'

When Spencer put the phone down, Morgan realised he'd been kippered. For a few uncharacteristic moments he had to fight off a surge of rising panic, until he thought of ringing his old boss and mentor, Kelvin Mackenzie. He blathered out the story and asked him what he should do.

Kelvin listened and considered before answering. 'That,' he said slowly but firmly, 'sounds like a disgusting attempt by Earl Spencer to con *News of the World* readers, using his wife and kids to do it.' That was all Piers needed. He rushed over to the back bench, epicentre of the paper's production department and told the startled subs what had happened, ordering them to change the front-page headline to:

"WHAT A CHARLIE!
Althorp invents pack of lies about wife and kids to trick *News of the World* readers."

For once, other papers and the television stations took the side of the *News of the World*. Spencer's cleverly constructed ruse proved to be a little too smart for its own good, having turned round and kicked him in the soft bits. It must have been a delicious moment for the young editor. Clive Goodman's little letter had turned out a gem, after all – for a while, at least.

Spencer subsequently regained some satisfaction when he and Victoria, from whom he was by then divorced, lodged a complaint with the PCC concerning photographs of her walking in the grounds of a detoxification clinic along with more details of the couple's marital problems. The PCC ruled that this action ran contrary to the editors' code of conduct, and reprimanded Morgan, while Earl Spencer took the opportunity to speak about his anguish shortly afterwards. 'Somebody has got to make it clear to the tabloids that they cannot go on behaving in this way,' he said. 'They've got no right to trample on people's most private life. I think this is a victory for those who believe the tabloids often go completely too far.'

In an unexpected *volte face*, even some of the strongest advocates of the tabloid press now appeared to agree with him. The *News of the World* had printed the most intrusive coverage. Rupert Murdoch publicly rebuked Morgan and issued a statement close to an apology. 'This company will not tolerate its papers bringing into disrepute the best practices of popular journalism,' he said. It was rumoured that he asked Piers to go. However, in *The Insider* Morgan says that he left of his own accord and somewhat against Murdoch's wishes, when he was offered the job of editor at the *Daily Mirror*.

Morgan was replaced as editor by Phil Hall. Hall had joined *The People* in 1985, and over seven years on the title he'd worked as chief reporter and news editor. In 1993 he spent a year at the *Sunday Express*, also as news editor, before arriving at Wapping to begin a seven-year stint on the *News of the World*. Upon his appointment as editor of the paper, Piers Morgan, to his colleagues' surprise, named Hall, then a member of the features desk, as his number two, because Hall had always been good to Matt Oliver, a freelance contributor on the *People* who also happened to be Morgan's grandfather. Piers claimed, with touching grandfilial loyalty, 'Anyone my grandfather trusts I can trust.'

Hall remained in the editor's chair for five years, breaking stories about the 'Drug Shame' of England rugby star Lawrence Dallaglio; "London's Burning" actor, John Alford; and harmless young peer, Jo, Earl of Hardwicke. He also signed up the octuplets' mother Mandy Allwood. Many of the biggest stories in his tenure were attributable to investigative 'ace' Mazher Mahmood, who the paper claimed had put over a hundred crooks in jail. Phil also fell for the powerful charms of Princess Diana, and when the paper caught her out with her secret love Hasnet Khan, Hall allowed her to persuade him that, despite her suspicious 3am departure from his flat, she was merely interested in Khan's work. Phil's not especially glorious reign came to an end in 2000, when he went and became Editor-in-Chief of *Hello!* He wasn't much missed at the *Screws* and was replaced by Rebekah Wade.

Wade had been one of Piers Morgan's loyal cohorts during his two-year stint at the *News of the World* in 1994-95. He loved her chutzpah and forthright grittiness, and she'd been beside him on a lot of his major stories. She says she decided to become a journalist when she was only 14, and opened her career on *Architecture Aujourd'hui* in Paris, making use of her fluent French. She returned to Cheshire, where she'd grown up, to work for Eddie Shah's Messenger Group and, later, his *Post* newspaper.

At 22, Rebekah got her first taste of life at the *News of the World* when she joined its *Sunday* magazine as a secretary. From there she worked her way up through the ranks to become deputy editor under Phil Hall, before being sent to *The Sun* in 1998 as David Yelland's deputy. In this job, she openly voiced her hostility to the long-standing tradition of the Page 3 Girls. She didn't get a result then, but she did gain influential allies through Women in Journalism. (Ten years later, appearing as editor of *The Sun* before a House of Lords committee, she vigorously defended the topless models who still appear on Page 3, saying that 7.7 million male and female readers of her paper 'loved' the traditional feature.)

In May 2000, at the age of 31, she was appointed the third female editor of the *News of the World* and one of the youngest (though not *the* youngest, Piers Morgan couldn't help pointing out when he rang to congratulate her). Rebekah was anxious to make her mark and her reign at the *Screws* was frequently controversial. After the murder of schoolgirl Sarah Payne, Wade took the risky, and it turned out, ill-advised step of publishing the names and photographs of known sex-offenders in order to 'protect other children from them'.

The public took her exhortations on board and set about hunting down paedophiles like Shires toffs after foxes. Mobs ran riot, and the paedophiles were forced back underground – which was to no-one's advantage. Tony Butler, Chief Constable of Gloucestershire, denounced her for 'grossly irresponsible' journalism, and the broadsheets accused her of trying to cash in on Sarah's murder. But Rebekah had struck a chord, she'd whipped up the parents' fear, and after a period of drifting sales, the *News of the World* added back an extra 95,000 copies. That was what really mattered, and Rebekah was making her mark.

Wade was editor of the paper on September 11 2001, one of the most notable dates in modern history. The date is notable, too, in the annals of the *News of the World*, though for other, lesser events that clearly illustrated the extraordinary, detached culture the paper had developed after seven years of peddling celebrity trivia.

At this time, Harry Potter mania was up and running like a golden hare, and in Wade's eyes, this merited a dedicated Harry Potter correspondent. It had been drawn to her attention that in the newsroom was an earnest 29-year-old journalist called Charles Begley

Later in the day, Begley was rung by Greg Miskiw, the assistant editor (news) (who had been away the week of September 11th).

'I've heard you're ill,' Greg said. 'What's the problem?'

Begley told Miskiw what he'd told Kuttner earlier in the day. 'Neville (Thurlbeck) got a message from Rebekah asking me to dress up in my Potter gear and go to her office. I think Neville was as surprised as I was. I just couldn't bring myself to prance about as Harry Potter when something like 50,000 people were dead.'

'I understand where you're coming from. You want to be taken seriously as a journalist; you don't want to be prancing around doing silly things.'

'I'm not being precious,' Begley assured him. 'I toed along with it as far as possible. I didn't walk out there and then, but I have to say I was tempted.'

'Well, if I'd have been there, I would have said to her, "Look, he can't..." Ah, well. You said two things?'

'I heard more great Harry Potter scenarios are planned. I'd be in Hollywood prancing around, while Stuart White [*News of the World*'s American editor] and I don't know who else would be in New York doing proper stuff. I would be dressed up as a transvestite teenage schoolboy, for God's sake! I did it for as long as I could. It's a shame because I'd worked hard to get my job. But I couldn't do it again.'

'OK,' Greg said.

'I'm sorry you've been left to deal with it, because I'm sure you're faced with a bit of an inquisition on it. I'm not trying to swing the lead.'

'I hear what you're saying, Charles. When I went in to talk to Rebekah this morning, she was concerned this had happened. It was mentioned if it was this Harry Potter thing. At that point, I didn't know about all this. So, what do you want me to do with this information?'

'Well, she should know. She should be aware of it. I don't want to criticise her in a phone call, but I can't see how the editor of the – as we're always reminded – "best paper in the country", could expect a reporter to do that. I'm not being precious – I know we have to do silly things. It was hardly appropriate and it was bloody humiliating. That was just too much.'

'I hear you. Let me speak to Stuart.'

Later that day, Greg Miskiw called Charles Begley again.

'Stuart would like to know what your plans are. Now, we don't want to lose you. I'm not asking you to come in tomorrow. Come in on Friday. We had this problem, and we sorted it out. We are taking this serious, in the sense of how it's affected you. Rebekah has heard what you've said, and accepts what you're saying. Stuart has heard what you've said, and accepts what you're saying. But saying "I'll call you tomorrow" is not really acceptable.'

'I'm thinking to myself that my situation now was that my copy book was completely blotted.'

'It's not. I don't want you to think that. What you need to do is pick yourself up, dust yourself down, and say: "Fuck it". Rebekah's said: Right, let's get him off the Harry Potter thing. Let's get him to change back to his real name.'

'Obviously, I do want to come back to work, but if I just rush back in....'

'We really don't want to put any pressure on you,' Greg murmured solicitously.

'I find it hard to believe that for the editor's pet project to crumble away in such a spectacular fashion isn't going to be held against me in any way.'

'Listen Charles, I decide who goes out on jobs. If a good story comes in on Friday, I'm going to put you on it. I promise you, I'm giving you good advice here. I can't afford to lose someone of your calibre.'

Begley agreed to call Miskiw back in an hour.

'I don't think I can make a final decision on my future right now,' he told Miskiw.

'I'm not forcing you into a decision,' Miskiw said. 'I'm telling you something that will benefit you.'

'I'm so wound up about all this.'

'Charles, Charles, Charles, let me tell you something. This is not a business for prima donnas. You know that and I know that.'

'I'm disillusioned...' Begley protested.

'I've told you that this isn't going to be held against you. Charles, you should think very seriously about coming in on Tuesday.'

'Well, to be frank, Greg, as far as my future at News International is concerned, I haven't toed the line for the editor's pet project. I didn't prance around while the World Trade Centre was being bombed for her personal amusement. I can't just stroll in.'

'Why not?' Greg urged him. 'Charles, that is what we do – we go out and destroy other people's lives.'

Charles Begley left the *News of the World* – and nothing changed. Over many years the paper has set out deliberately and without compassion to destroy other people's lives in order to sell newspapers. The supreme discomfort of others is meat and drink to the paper, and the extent to which they hurt people concerns them only as far as the cost of any damages that might subsequently be claimed. Cynical judgements are made about the price of knowingly committing some actionable offence, assessing what a likely settlement would be, and balancing that against the anticipated increase in sales.

Piers Morgan recounts cheerfully in *The Insider* how when faced with a possible action for breach of copyright from the Mail on Sunday for lifting (effectively stealing) an exclusive interview with Will Carling and his wife, he calls across the newsroom to Tom Crone.

'Hey Tom, how many fingers will this cost us if we nick it all?'

Crone flicked five fingers at him – £50,000 maximum damages.

Fifty grand would have been well worth paying for a front page and two spreads inside – and the bigger sales revenue it would bring.

To the *News of the World*, anyone is fair game, irrespective of the hugely disproportionate damage its victim might suffer when set against what is often an entirely legal and completely *private* act, where no one else has been harmed. In the case of revealing illicit love affairs it is often the case that a potential injured party – an unknowing wife for example – will be substantially more hurt by the *public* revelation of her husband's infidelity than by the act itself. In revealing it, no wrong is being righted and no public interest is being served, beyond the titillation of the readers. Meanwhile, several people's lives are irreparably damaged.

Take the case of Arnold Lewis, a maths teacher, as reported by the News of the World in October 1978. Lewis had put an advertisement in a contact magazine, saying, 'Join our Welsh hills picnic party for remote rural rambles and shining summer scenes. Pub social meeting first.'

No doubt the nature of the magazine allowed readers to decode the precise purpose of this gathering. It struck a chord somewhere in the *Screws* newsroom, and two reporters were despatched to see what might be in store for any hopeful ramblers. At the meeting point there were only Mr Lewis, another couple and the intrepid reporters. They were led up a lane to Mr Lewis's caravan, where they were offered sherry, with chocolate biscuits, and pornographic magazines were laid out on a table. An open drawer revealed neatly arranged condoms. Mr Lewis explained that his wife wasn't there because she wasn't part of his swinging activities. She thought he went motor rallying at weekends, though he wished she were there too. After a little discussion about the non-emotional nature of wife-swapping, the reporters declined the offer to join in, and left the three consenting adults to get on with what is, though not to everyone's taste, a perfectly legal activity, which Mr Lewis had disguised from his wife so as not to upset her.

Two days before the report appeared in the paper, Tina Dalgleish, who had written the story, phoned Mr Lewis, as was customary, to inform him that it would be in the next edition of the paper.

That Sunday morning Arnold Lewis's body was found in his car. He had killed himself by inhaling exhaust fumes. He was 52.

At the inquest, counsel read Mr Lewis's suicide note, and asked Tina Dalgleish, 'Does that not upset you?'

'No not really. I can see that it might upset his wife, but it doesn't upset me.'

The editor at the time was Bernard Shrimsley, who in an interview with Matt Engel in 1995 admitted, 'If we'd known what the result would be we wouldn't have done it.'

'Did you lose sleep over it?'

'I still do.'

The *Screws*' choice of victims can be puzzling, as in 1999, even when under the steadier hand of Phil Hall. Its reporters seem particularly to enjoy bringing down great British sporting heroes, relishing the process of lifting them from the back pages where they reign supreme to give them a serious kicking at the sharp end of the paper. One pictures them chanting the old rugby mantra, 'The bigger they are, the harder they fall!' And in recent years they haven't come much bigger than Lawrence Dallaglio.

The reasons for setting up a man like Dallaglio – a superb, popular and inspiring rugby player, then captain of the England team – are hard to fathom, yet with great gusto and skill, the *News of the World* hacks targeted him, lied to him, flattered him, plied him with booze, and waved fake contracts worth hundreds of thousands of pounds under his nose. They pushed and pushed until they got him drunk enough to say something really stupid. Then they splashed it over the first five pages of their paper under the front-page headline:

"ENGLAND RUGBY CAPTAIN EXPOSED AS DRUG DEALER."

This, of course, turned out to be completely untrue. It was all the result of an elaborate con trick, and it was a downright lie to describe Dallaglio as a drug dealer. At no stage did the reporters witness a single transaction, or produce any other corroboration to support their contention. They had based it entirely on the hapless Dallaglio's own drunken, fantastical braggadocio.

Two reporters, Louise Oswald and Phil Taylor, conspired to entrap Lawrence by contacting Ashley Woolfe, his agent, through an individual named Peter Simmons, who purported to be creative director of an advertising agency, CSR Partnership. Masquerading as executives of the Gillette razor company, the reporters told Ashley that they wanted to use Lawrence's image for a major promotion of their Mach 3 razor. The money they were offering (£500,000 over two years) was enormous for a professional rugby player, whose wages are nothing like as extravagant as those of a footballer at a comparable level.

Over two or three well-lubricated dinners at Langan's and drinks galore in a private room at the Holland Park Hilton, the reporters built up his trust in them. Peter Simmons told him that the managing director of Gillette, 'James Tunstall' and his PA, 'Louise Wood', were real party animals who were expecting to have a 'good time' with him. Lawrence was an obliging sort of man, and he obliged by playing up to them in the way he thought they wanted him to. In a not uncommon scenario, the drunker he became, the more spectacular his bullshit became, and he started making up stories that gave the impression he was far more involved in drugs than he ever really was.

It was not an admirable way for England's Rugby captain to behave, but he felt he was expected to give them some bang for their buck – to shock them a little – and they did all they could to encourage him. Later, in their front-page piece, the reporters described with characteristic Screws faux primness how he had confessed to "astonished *News of the World* investigators".

"Delighted" might have been more accurate than "astonished": Lawrence had said exactly the kind of things they'd hoped he would say, for there can be no doubt they pick their marks with great care, especially when expense is involved, and they would have had a very good idea of who would sing and who wouldn't. Lawrence is a big, ebullient, outgoing, boastful character, which is what made him such a great captain of England's rugby team, but it was exactly these qualities that made him likely to be susceptible to this kind of sting.

The five-page splash came out on Sunday May 23, 1999, on a weekend when Lawrence and his partner, Alice Corbett, were having a relaxing, away-from-it-all break with their two daughters, Ella and two-week old Josie, specially to give Alice a chance to get over giving birth. They were staying in the Woolley Grange Hotel, an idyllic Jacobean manor house in Bradford-on-Avon, near Bath. Lawrence came down to breakfast before Alice and the girls, and immediately noticed a palpable sense of awkwardness. He was used to people noticing him, but usually with smiles, not shifty sideways glances.

He turned on his mobile to find a couple of missed calls, both from Ashley Woolfe, whom he immediately called back. Ashley wasted no time telling him he was all over the *News of the World*, that the people he thought were from Gillette were reporters from the paper.

Lawrence felt the world disintegrating around him. He was numb with panic, but he had to go back upstairs to tell Alice what had happened. It must have been a harrowing experience, much nastier than any hammering on the rugby pitch for Lawrence. Used to being confidently in control, he now found himself in a situation where he had none – all made worse by the fact that he'd allowed it to happen by carelessly dropping his guard.

It was only now that he recalled a couple of occasions when people had said there were rumours going around that he was going to be subject of a press sting, but with rugby on the back burner in the papers until the next tour, he'd thought the danger had long since passed. And now this had happened, he thought, because he'd got carried away on a deluge of drunken bullshit to impress these bastards who had utterly duped him. He felt a complete fool, and totally ashamed of himself for being taken in. Luckily, he had good friends, starting with his boss, England coach Clive Woodward, and after a hasty exit from the hotel, he and his family drove straight there, where they were welcomed with genuine warmth and understanding.

As months passed, the shock of the *News of the World*'s sting subsided, but repercussions went on for months as rugby officialdom felt it had to respond. In the end Lawrence was to appear at a quasi-legal hearing, for which George Carman agreed to represent him.

Meanwhile, the paper, vigorously defending itself against a torrent of abuse from the rest of the media, were humbled by seeing their headlined allegation that Dallaglio had been a drugs dealer utterly rubbished. The police took no action, and the RFU only took him to task for having used a small quantity of cocaine and some cannabis on one of the tours. He was also charged with the more nebulous offence of bringing the game into disrepute.

The RFU fined him £25,000, but, according to Dallaglio in his own book, *It's in the Blood*, that sum was circuitously repaid to him six months later. The net result of this vicious sting and the story it produced for the *News of the World*, was pain for Lawrence Dallaglio and his family and damaged morale for the English rugby team. The only benefit was a slight uplift in sales for the *News of the World*, and a nugatory increase in its profits to offset the losses made by their sibling *The Times*.

In 2005, the *News of the World* was given an award for *Scoop of the Year*, byline: Neville 'Onan' Thurlbeck. This was for the life-enhancing tale of a footballer's short-lived dalliance with his personal assistant in Madrid, a story which the paper splashed mightily April 4, 2004 and continued to run for the next few months. With awards like these, arcane in the criteria of their selection, it sometimes seems that the named journalist has had very little to do with the uncovering of the facts beyond converting the ramblings of their informant into tabloid speak.

In this case, the woman involved, Rebecca Loos, approached Max Clifford and asked him to sell to the highest bidder the story of her affair with David Beckham. Max knew that *News of the World* editor Andy Coulson would pay the most. Thurlbeck flew off to Spain to check the quality, and there it was – one of the juiciest tabloid stories of the year, and a deal was done. For two weeks, Rebecca and Thurlbeck were holed up in a secret villa outside Marbella. Thurlbeck used his years of experience in handling sexual scandals to squeeze every last titillating drop out of the story, especially the explicit details of how Beckham had performed as a lover.

When the story broke, Beckham – famously a man of few words – said it was 'ludicrous', although after it had appeared he did not seek redress through the libel courts. Besides, Rebecca had been very complimentary about his sexual prowess – making it the kind of story few men would want to rubbish.

Rebecca, to whom Thurlbeck attributed the absurd quote, 'I am afraid I have no comment for you. Please leave me alone', was rewarded with a sum of £300,000 or £800,000, depending on whom you believe. If she ever said it at all, one must assume it was before she got the wonga.

As an additional insult to his readers' intelligence, Onan added another quote from 'Rebecca's friend'.

'Rebecca is heartbroken this story has come out, but she knew it would eventually. Too many people have seen her texts and they've got into the wrong hands.'

Oh dear, poor little Rebecca!

Naughty old Onan.

One must accept, I suppose, that the public is genuinely fascinated by the prurient details of their sporting heroes' sex-lives, and Roy Greenslade told the BBC that in his view there hadn't been a bigger story since the serialisation of Andrew Morton's book about Princess Diana in *The Sunday Times* in 1992.

The tabloids had a feeding frenzy on that, but with the death of Diana they have elevated the Beckhams into her slot, in the way that they can ramp up their sales. They have elevated them – and the Beckhams have elevated themselves to a dizzying height of fame. In British terms they are the most famous couple in the country, whether we like it or not. That makes the alleged fall from grace even more significant, and the 'Red Tops' all the more gleeful. Negative news always gives much more pleasure to the tabloid newspapers than positive news.

Many might say that the Beckhams have courted the media so slavishly, they are more than fair game to the press who feed on them; others will respond that it must certainly have been a horrible experience for David and Victoria, who, despite the evidence, are real people with real feelings, and anxious, like most of us, to keep relationships intact and thriving. But that a news item of such triviality should have pushed, say, events in war-torn Iraq right off the front pages is alarming to anyone who cares about the valid propagation of news.

Rebecca Loos' £300,000+ pay-out was one of the more extravagant examples of what the 'Red Tops' will pay for a major kiss-&-tell splash, but making big payments for big stories (so-called 'chequebook journalism') is a well-established practice in tabloid journalism. One of the obvious advantages is that once a kiss-&-teller can smell the big money under their nose, they're ready to say whatever they thinks the journalist wants to hear. To make sure of their story, the papers nearly always specify in their contracts that the money will be paid only on publication, thereby encouraging subjects to embellish and embroider until an editor has just the story he wants. In early 2007, this cynical type of journalism was clearly visible in a story about the Duke of Westminster.

Splashed across five pages on a Sunday in February, the *News of the World* alleged that the Duke had hired a number of prostitutes to visit him at his home in Mayfair. They published pictures of girls supposedly leaving his house, beneath explicit headlines about how he had paid them in cash for their services. To the reader, it appeared as just another good, old-fashioned exposé of shenanigans in high places.

However, closer investigation reveals the *News of the World*'s version to be a far less clear scenario. After careful reading of the whole article, it is apparent that only one of the call girls described, a 26-year-old Lithuanian named Zana Brazdek, alleged in an interview that she had visited the Duke. Once the story was published, and only then, Zana was paid the sum of £25,000, transferred to her bank by the *News of the World*.

But what could the Duke do about this? By all accounts a modest, genial man, he was obliged to carry on his family life in the full glare of the vivid allegations the paper had made, irrespective of whether or not they were true.

It has been shown with a number of high-profile but essentially blameless individuals who have been damaged by the tabloids that going to the courts to seek some kind of fair redress involves the minute dissection of every detail that has appeared, true or false, often over weeks in the High Court, slavishly reported by the same tabloids that have instigated the damage in the first place. Canny editors, and lawyers like Tom Crone at News International, know that even if a story is based on very flimsy premises, it is often simply not worth a victim's while to prolong the agony of ongoing publicity.

It's significant, too, that the story of the Duke of Westminster was constructed during the last weeks of Andy Coulson's editorship, and appeared two weeks after he resigned. Something very big was needed to distract public attention away from Clive Goodman's conviction and jailing, although the blurring of fact and fiction turned out to have been the principal characteristic of much of Coulson's inglorious reign at Wapping.

Andy Coulson was 35 in 2003 when Rupert Murdoch appointed him Editor of the *News of the World* to replace Rebekah Wade, whom he'd promoted to edit *The Sun*. Like former editor Piers Morgan, Coulson was an alumnus of the school of celebrity gossip that was the *Bizarre* page of *The Sun*. His journey to the top of the stack had been rapid but surprised no one.

Andy was born on January 21, 1968 and spent his earliest years in his parent's council house in Basildon, until they moved to Wickford, in the flatlands of Essex. At the age of 11 he started at his local school, Beauchamps Comprehensive, now Beauchamps High School and well regarded. Bright, but not especially academic, Andy stayed there for 7 years before leaving to do the job he'd always wanted to do.

Successful in his application for a reporter's traineeship on the *Basildon Evening Echo*, he learned the ropes very swiftly. In two years he'd gathered enough experience to break free and pitch for a job as a freelancer on the *Sun's Bizarre* showbiz page. Then-editor Piers Morgan, three years his senior, took him on and became a good friend.

Andy immediately stood out in this environment, showing a natural talent for prising open the private lives of the celebrities who were the page's staple. So impressive was he that the *Daily Mail's* Ian Monk rated him the best of the young showbiz hacks in London and poached him in 1994.

Andy crossed London to the unfamiliar ambience of Kensington and the *Mail* newsroom, to remain there a mere nine weeks before *The Sun* enticed him back to Wapping to edit *Bizarre*. Upon his return to *The Sun*, he quickly consolidated his position and widely expanded his contacts among the showbiz press officers with tireless networking. In 1998 he was also made an associate editor of the paper; clearly great things were expected of him. (Andy also showed an occasional taste for mischief, and once fed a bogus story to the rival *Mirror* that Paula Yates was having a rib removed, for cosmetic reasons.)

After four years spent laying a very solid base to his career, Coulson was moved by News International to be Editorial Director of News Network, News International's internet arm – which, like similar departments at all newspapers, was destined to become a vital component of the paper. In 2000 he was promoted deputy editor of the *News of the World* under Rebekah Wade, and when she went off to edit *The Sun* in 2003, he moved into her still-warm chair.

Once he'd bedded in, despite his comparative youth, he was perceived as personable, charming and a relatively relaxed editor who was popular with his staff. He personally kept a low profile, seldom gave interviews and gave no sign of hankering after the limelight like his peer and friend Piers Morgan. For a while there was an assumption in Fleet Street that Andy Coulson would eventually succeed Rebekah at *The Sun* or get kicked up into a major management job at News International, at which he would have been highly competent.

In the course of his stewardship of the *News of the World*, Andy saw a few great successes (by tabloid standards) but also some major disasters. There's no doubt that he scored with several iconic scoops and won Newspaper of the Year at the 2005 British Press Awards, along with their Best Scoop award for the Beckham/Loos story. (Whether or not he shared this privately with Max Clifford is not recorded). He told the Press Gazette:

> I've got nothing to be ashamed of, and this goes for everyone on the *News of the World*, in what we do for a living. The readers are the judges – that's the most important thing. The *News of the World* doesn't pretend to do anything other than reveal big stories and titillate and entertain the public, while exposing crime and hypocrisy.

The previous year he was rumoured to have rejected an approach to edit the *Daily Mirror* after Piers Morgan was sacked for publishing fake pictures of British troops abusing Iraqi prisoners.

In the autumn of 2005, just before the annual Tory Party Conference, Coulson apparently showed his otherwise obscure political colours by running a front-page splash ...

"TOP TORY, COKE AND THE HOOKER"

Illustrated with pictures of the angel-faced Shadow Chancellor, George Osborne, the story claimed that eleven years earlier, the virtually flawless Osborne was said, without any convincing corroboration, to have been watched by 'dominatrix' hooker, Natalie

Rowe, snorting a line of coke. Her boyfriend, an unnamed friend of Osborne's, had gone on to become an addict, the report alleged.

It was, on closer inspection, an archetypal Screws non-story – devoid of any hard content, carefully worded to avoid any serious come-back, but just salacious enough to justify its front-page status. The only 'revelation' it contained about the politician was the fact that in his youth he'd had a friend who knew a prostitute and who'd become addicted to an unspecified drug.

In February 2006, Andy scored a truly vicious scoop when the paper revealed that Liberal Democrat MP Mark Oaten had paid for the sexual services of a male prostitute over a six-month period. According to many of his constituents, Oaten was a competent, conscientious and industrious Member of Parliament whose sexual preferences had no bearing whatever on his value as their MP. While some felt he had shown dishonesty in not revealing his sexuality, others were disgusted that such an able man was forced to resign his job as Lib Dem Home Affairs spokesman and would not stand again for election as a result of one tabloid rag's spiteful, homophobic attack. In either case the life of this otherwise decent man wasn't simply made temporarily uncomfortable; it will never be the same again. Nevertheless, in the spring of that year, Coulson once again came back from the London Press Club Awards clutching prizes, for – among other things – the exposé of the former Home Secretary, David Blunkett's affair with *Spectator* publisher, Kimberly Quinn. But as the year ground on, for the *News of the World* it began to take on the characteristics of an *annus horribilis*.

CHAPTER FOUR

A YEAR OF PAIN FOR ANDY COULSON

Murdoch's star Sunday sheet had been named Sunday Newspaper of the Year for the third year running in 2006. By what criteria the industry judges and awards itself is a mystery to most outsiders, but whatever the reasons, by the end of the year, the paper was in bad trouble.

The disasters that had piled up during the second half of 2006 came to a head when the paper's top royal reporter and the contract private investigator it employed appeared in the Old Bailey to answer charges of extensive phone tapping into Prince Charles's household. To charges of conspiracy to intercept telephone calls 'without lawful authority' between 1 November, 2005 and 9 August, 2006 Clive Goodman pleaded guilty – no doubt providing great relief for his bosses, who must have feared the revelations that a long trial would have unearthed.

As Clive sat in the dock, pale and fiddling nervously, John Kelsey-Fry QC, who appeared for him, addressed the judge. 'Clive Goodman wishes, through me, to take the first opportunity to apologise publicly to those affected by his actions. He accepts they were a gross invasion of privacy.

'He therefore apologises unreservedly to the three members of the Royal Household staff concerned and their principals, Prince William, Prince Harry and the Prince of Wales.'

Mr Justice Gross replied, on the matter of sentencing, 'I am not ruling out any options.'

Clive Goodman was remanded on unconditional bail for pre-sentence reports.

Glenn Mulcaire pleaded guilty to the same offence as well as five further charges of unlawfully intercepting voice-mail messages left by the publicist Max Clifford; the footballer Sol Campbell's agent, Skylet Andrew; chairman of the Professional Footballers Association, Gordon Taylor; the MP Simon Hughes and the model Elle Macpherson. Fourteen other 'alternative' charges which both Goodman and Mulcaire originally faced were ordered to be left on the file.

After the hearing Max Clifford said he wasn't surprised to discover his calls were being tapped, commenting:

Clive Goodman has been caught doing something which is becoming far more widespread in tabloid journalism in recent years,' he said. 'I suppose the only way you can justify this kind of activity is when the end product is genuinely something the nation can benefit from, something to do with national security. If by tapping people's phones, you save people's lives and you can stop some national tragedy, then the end justifies the means. But for tittle-tattle and gossip, then the end does not justify the means.'

Editor Andy Coulson also offered his unreserved apologies on behalf of the *News of the World* to all parties involved for the distress caused by the invasion of their privacy.

'As the editor of the newspaper,' he went said. 'I take ultimate responsibility for the conduct of my reporters. Clive Goodman's actions were entirely wrong and I have put in place measures to ensure that they will not be repeated by any member of my staff.

'I have also written today to Sir Michael Peat, the Prince of Wales's private secretary, to this effect. The *News of the World* will also be making a substantial donation to charities of the princes' choice.'

Sir Christopher Meyer, the chairman of the Press Complaints Commission, said that the commission's journalistic code of practice was absolutely clear on the issue of phone message tapping. 'It is a totally unacceptable practice unless there is a compelling public interest reason for carrying it out. In this case, a crime has been committed as well – something which I deplore.'

On January 26, 2007 Clive Goodman appeared before The Honourable Mr Justice Gross once again, this time for sentencing. Alongside him stood his outside contractor, Glenn 'Trigger' Mulcaire, at the bottom of a messy heap of News International employees whom many thought would have been implicated but claimed complete ignorance of what had happened.

Goodman had admitted making 487 calls to the private mobile phone voicemail message services of three royal aides. He had made the calls from a landline at News International premises, on his own mobile phone, and from a landline registered in his own name at his home in Putney. On a single count of conspiracy to intercept communications contrary to section (1) 1 of the 1977 Criminal Law Act, which merited a maximum of two years, the judge sentenced him to four months in jail, not a terrifically long stretch, but easily long enough to cripple a man's self-esteem and stain his reputation for many years.

Glenn Mulcaire had also pleaded guilty to conspiracy charges brought under the Criminal Law Act, as well as eight substantive offences of unlawful interception of communications contrary to section 1(1) of the Regulation of Investigatory Powers Act 2000. To achieve these interceptions, Mulcaire had relied mainly on the old-fashioned art of 'blagging'. It emerged that once Clive Goodman had passed him the mobile numbers he was to target, Mulcaire would frequently call O_2 Customer Services. The investigating police had obtained seven recordings of him posing as an employee of O_2 credit control department. Using the alias Paul Williams and a company password which was regularly changed, he was heard asking the customer services representatives to reset to default the PIN codes for Paddy Harverson's and Helen Asprey's voicemail. The police were unable to establish how Mulcaire had access to the passwords, and no inside employee at O_2 was implicated.

Mulcaire had gone through a similar process with Vodafone to reset the PIN to default for Jamie Lowther-Pinkerton's mobile voicemail. Mulcaire was also found to have accessed the voicemails of a number of other individuals, not for Clive Goodman, but for other *News of the World* staff. For these, he had accessed and listened to messages himself.

One of his targets was Max Clifford, who'd recently had a row with News of the World editor Andy Coulson about the paper running a damning exposé of former Atomic Kitten, Kerry Katona. Ever loyal to his clients, Max had "frozen out" Coulson and not given him another story since. No doubt there were those in Wapping who were very anxious to know what he was up to. But Max Clifford is a very wary chap, and there is no record of any story escaping his carefully guarded net.

Mulcaire's retainer from News International of £2,019 per week, plus (as 'Alexander') a weekly cash payment of £500 (£12,300 in all) from Clive Goodman's expenses had been revealed in the hearing. The payments were alleged primarily to have been for passing on information from these sources, although the newspaper management maintained it was for a wide range of other legitimate research services he provided, including football knowledge.

Goodman and Mulcaire had also managed to tap directly into the princes' mobile numbers. This was evident from the very explicit story in April 2006 of the voicemail left for Prince Harry by Prince William, pretending to be an angry Chelsy, memorably headlined:

"FURY AFTER HE OGLED LAPDANCERS' BOOBS"

Neville Thurlbeck had also been a party to this story – at least to the extent that his by-line had appeared over it with Goodman's. What no one at Wapping knew was that the police had been monitoring messages on the Clarence House voicemails and comparing them with stories appearing in the *News of the World* for the past four months. Clarence House must have been expecting the story to appear, and one can imagine their amusement when they saw what Goodman probably thought was his best phone-tapped story duly pop up.

However, Thurlbeck was never arrested or charged in connection with this particular illegal interception, and nothing is known about what he knew of its origins. Nor, as it happened, were Goodman or

Mulcaire charged, since it had been decided to charge them only with the tapping of the staff phones, from which more than enough had been gleaned to justify the arrest and successful prosecution of the parties involved. This would also dispose of the need to drag the princes themselves into court.

Despite the early 'guilty' pleas registered by Goodman and Mulcaire and their co-operation with the police investigation, the judge indicated that the identity of their targets made a custodial sentence essential. In his summing up his lordship made it clear that neither journalists nor private security consultants were above the law.

'This case', he said, 'is not, and has not been suggested to be in any sense, about press freedom. It is about grave, inexcusable and illegal invasion of privacy. This was not pushing at the limits or on the cusp. What you did was plainly on the wrong side of the line.

'It is essential for the decency of our public life that conduct of this nature is clearly marked as unacceptable and is discouraged by sentences which demonstrate unambiguously that the game is not worth the candle.

'The targets here were members of the Royal Family, through the individuals of the Royal Household whose voicemails were accessed. The Royal Family, of course, holds a unique position in the life of this country. That is by itself grave indeed, but matters do not end there. The threat such conduct poses is a threat to all engaged in public life.'

Clive Goodman was taken down and off to Belmarsh maximum security prison to begin his sentence (where he was reported to be sharing a cell with a lifer). He was later moved to the marginally less harsh surroundings of HM Prison, Swaleside on the Isle of Sheppey, where at least half the inmates were lifers.

It cannot have been a cheering sight for the former royal editor as he stood shivering and gazed through the mesh across the flat, featureless marshes as the winter wind blew off a cold North Sea in this isolated corner of Kent, not far from where he had started his journalistic career on the *Kentish Times*. From where he stood the prospect could not have been bleaker. He was humiliated, disgraced and unemployable. He'd instructed agents to sell his house to pay his legal costs and fund his living expenses until such time as he was able to find another job. And his only daughter wasn't yet two.

The *News of the World*'s own report of Goodman's sentence was delivered with characteristic lack of accuracy in an effort to play down the scale of his crime. Their royal editor, they reported, 'has been jailed for four months for plotting to hack into the phone messages of royal aides.' They couldn't even muster enough honesty to admit that he hadn't just plotted, he'd actually done it, 487 times!

***

Back in Wapping, shortly after 6.00pm on the day Goodman's jail sentence had been handed down, the *News of the World* staff assembled to be addressed by their editor Andy Coulson.

Handsome, charming and unstoppably on the rise, Coulson appeared wearing one of his conventional three-button suits and an air of detached professionalism. Andy had never employed the same management techniques as the more rambunctious (not to say foulmouthed) editors of Murdoch's 'Red Tops'. Still only 37, he was always in quiet and firm control of the eclectic rabble that customarily inhabits the newsroom of a national tabloid, never resorting to the all-out, bare-arsed public bollockings, which Kelvin Mackenzie of *The Sun* had famously dealt out in the Wapping compound in former years.

Now, in a brief but highly charged farewell, Coulson told his staff he was resigning, with immediate effect, the chair he had occupied for the past four years and thanked them for their loyalty. He took the opportunity to vent his anger at the sentence, railing that just that week the Home Secretary, John Reid, had advised judges, in view of current prison overcrowding, that only the most dangerous criminals should be sent to prison. With a convincing display of bitterness from the man who had championed Megan's Law – designed to identify convicted paedophiles – he pointed out, with standard *News of the World* disregard for precise relevance, that Goodman's sentence came the same day a judge had spared – well, not an actual paedophile, but a child porn downloader – from jail, for reasons of overcrowding.

Coulson could have resigned sooner – when the charges were laid, when Goodman and Mulcaire pleaded guilty two months before – but it seems likely he'd been waiting to see how harshly the judge would come down on his underling. Perhaps if Goodman hadn't been sent down, Coulson's remorse at the part he had played would have been commensurately less and he wouldn't have found it necessary to quit. (Although, in career terms, it would have meant he would not have been available to take up a prestigious and lucrative job advising David Cameron on how to outbounce Gordon Brown.)

In any case, his resignation prevented the PCC from quizzing him over the Goodman affair (as he had 'left the industry'), so no one can be sure exactly how much he knew about it. To be just, his statement of resignation had admitted 'ultimate responsibility' for Goodman's actions and, according to friends, Coulson himself descended into a deep depression in the weeks that followed. He cancelled his 39th birthday party at a West London hotel and retreated into his shell, emerging only to play a little golf near his home in Forest Hill.

One friend said he gave the impression that he was 'slightly disillusioned' about the whole *raison d'etre* of the *News of the World* towards the end of his editorship. This may be because, now a 'family man', he'd become more serious about life, and the kind of stories the paper was running were very much at odds with this. It's been observed, certainly, that since the birth of his two boys, Monty and Harvey, to his wife, Eloise, he has become a doting father – a process that tends to soften the most hardened of cynics.

That Coulson was appointed to the sensitive post of David Cameron's Spinner-in-Chief suggests that the received view in higher political circles is that Coulson was not aware of what Goodman had done. Certainly he made clear in a public statement that he felt that his royal editor's actions were 'entirely wrong', and went on to say, 'I deeply regret that they happened on my watch. I also feel strongly that when The *News of the World* calls those in public life to account on behalf of its readers, it must have its own house in order.'

But Coulson does have his doubters. To quote the *Guardian*'s John Harris, 'Some people, however, continue to believe that Mulcaire's work for the *News of the World* was so extensive and well-paid that the idea that Coulson was unaware of the phone-tapping beggars belief.'

Likewise, the House of Commons Select Committee on Culture, Media and Sport concluded a fairly damning report with the words: 'We find it extraordinary that in their investigation into the case, the Press Complaints Commission did not feel it necessary to question Mr Coulson on these points.' In other words, they thought he'd been lucky to have got away with it so easily. (They hadn't called Coulson either, by the way, which wasn't very brave of them.)

In addition to this, Andy Coulson's reign, despite the puzzling awards, was chequered almost from the start. Before his shameful debacle, his 'watch' had included an indecent number of incidents that must have embarrassed the editor of the nation's biggest selling paper. An early disaster occurred in June 2003, when the paper was at the centre of controversy about payments to witnesses after the collapse of the trial of five Eastern Europeans accused of plotting to kidnap Victoria Beckham and her children. The events that led to this had occurred in November 2002 under Rebekah Wade's leadership, while Andy Coulson had been her deputy, but he was left to face the brickbats when it all went wrong. On that occasion, unlike the later 'Red Mercury' trial, there had at least been the germ of a genuine conspiracy between a group of four Romanians and one Albanian to acquire a jewelled ceremonial turban that had been stolen from Sotheby's in London.

The principle author of the extraordinary story was the paper's star investigations editor, Mazher Mahmood, although the original idea for it had come from Florim Gashi, a 27-year-old Kosovan parking attendant who was one of Mazher's regular 'reliable' sources. For his first encounter with the gang Mazher adopted the pose of a rich potential buyer and arranged to meet them in a West London hotel. The apparent boss, Azem Krifsha, took him through to the hotel lavatory, where he revealed the turban and said he wanted £40,000 for it. Mazher, having arranged for an aide to film the event secretly, told them he would let them know and went back to consider what he had.

Mazher and his editor, Rebekah Wade decided that although it was a genuine crime, as no celebrity names were involved, it wasn't hot enough to run as it was. Maz returned to Gashi and told him that this was not a story that would sell newspapers, and the reasons why.

Gashi promptly mentioned that the gang had also looked at the possibility of kidnapping a Saudi prince who was in London, but he'd been too heavily guarded. This must have been a disappointment to Mazher; however, in order not to waste his contact with this compliant little gang, he went back and suggested that they start plotting instead to kidnap Victoria Beckham for £5 million. This switch to a celebrity-led story became clearer at the later Red Mercury trial, when Gashi told the court, 'Maz said I would get £10,000 and another £5,000 if they got prosecuted. I would get it if I could get them to talk about the kidnap of Victoria Beckham and her children.' Mazher also instructed Gashi secretly to tape all of these conversations.

One member of Mazher's investigations team was recruited as a getaway driver, and the gang was recorded discussing, in what turned out to be a desultory, unconvincing way, how they planned to break in to the Beckhams' house, ambush Victoria, disable her by spraying her with a chemical substance, and drive her to a safe house in Brixton where they would prepare a cell for her. If her sons were with her, they would just have to come too. The plotting hadn't gone far by the time Mazher decided to inform the police of the massive conspiracy he had unearthed; he needed to act before the team went off the boil and lost their enthusiasm, or simply realized that they were never going to get into the house in the first place.

In any event, the police came on board and after scouring the Beckhams' house for evidence (which was never found), on a Saturday morning officers from SO7, Scotland Yard's Serious and Organised Crime Command unit, arrested four men and a woman in raids – one, an armed raid in London's Docklands area, another in residential premises in Morden, South London. Another four people, including a second woman, were arrested in other operations late on Saturday and early on Sunday, the police announced. The nine were held for questioning at unnamed police stations across London.

One can only surmise that the timing of the raids on a Saturday was designed to protect the *News of the World*'s exclusivity, because on any other day of the week, the dailies would have had chance to pick up the story from the police and run it before Mazher had had his first bite.

On the Sunday, Rebekah Wade, no doubt with the tip of her tongue gently clenched between her lovely teeth, gave the story a spectacular full-bleed front-page splash:

"WORLD EXCLUSIVE! WE STOP THE CRIME OF THE CENTURY!"

Mazher Mahmood appeared, albeit unrecognisably, as one of the spread-eagled figures being covered by armed police at the place of arrest, where his photographer was conveniently located in a nearby building for the best possible overhead shots.

In Mazher's customary breathless prose, he reported how an 'international' gang's plot to kidnap Victoria Beckham had been cleverly foiled by the *News of the World*. Five of the plotters were charged with conspiracy and were to spend the next seven months on remand in prison.

Although the resultant court case revealed that the conspiracy had been little more than wishful thinking – like buying a ticket for the lottery to fantasise about winning the rollover jackpot – on the part of a few impoverished Eastern European migrants, at the time the police encouraged the Beckhams themselves to take the threat very seriously.

David was first informed about it after he'd just played a lacklustre game against Southampton in Manchester. He was walking back to the dressing room when Alex Ferguson told him they needed to talk in his office – at once. David lifted an eyebrow but complied and clattered into the room still wearing his kit and boots. To his surprise, Victoria was waiting for him, pale and nervous. He knew at once that something was very wrong. It was a moment before he even noticed there were four other people in the room. Beckham vaguely recognised a Manchester-based police officer who introduced the other three – members of SO7 who had just driven up from Scotland Yard. David waited for someone to tell him what the hell was going on. The gaffer told him to sit down and listen.

He could barely believe what he was hearing when they told him that following a tip-off from the *News of the World* they had just arrested nine people who had been planning to kidnap Victoria and the boys with the aim of extracting a ransom of £5 million. Victoria still looked very nervous at what appeared to have been a narrow escape. She did, though, manage to joke that they'd have to have kidnapped her hairdresser as well if they'd wanted any peace.

Nevertheless it was a massive shock to the footballer who famously and genuinely doted on his two boys and, as it would with any fond father and husband, the threat of this kind of abduction made his stomach churn. The police compounded his anxiety by saying that they had already posted officers outside the Beckhams' houses at Alderley Edge and Sawbridgeworth.

The next day David and Victoria couldn't stop themselves from reading Mazher Mahmood's graphic front-page story and watching all the attendant TV coverage; it was a very traumatic experience, knowing how close the threat had come to reality – or so they quite reasonably thought at the time.

They must have felt very sick a few months later when the trial of the 'conspirators' collapsed and revealed that rather than a full-blown kidnap plot there had been little more than a half-formed fantasy, used by Mahmood to get his by-line once again on the front page of the *News of the World*. Nevertheless, it's very hard for anyone to completely dismiss the idea of a threat like this once it's been planted and, still worried about it, the Beckhams sought advice from a wide field of experts and spent a great deal of money on security for their children.

Once the trial was abandoned and defence lawyers claimed the paper had shown 'complete contempt for the administration of justice', Judge Simon Smith referred to the role of the News of the World in the nurturing of the conspiracy to Lord Goldsmith, the Attorney General, 'to consider the temptations to which money being offered in return for stories may have a detrimental effect on court proceedings.' The *News of the World* jumped up and down, proclaiming self-righteously that it would continue to investigate any stories with a clear public interest.

The debacle of the Beckham kidnap trial was followed by a libel claim against the paper. Alin Turcu, just 18 at the time of his arrest and described by Mazher as the gang's 'surveillance expert', was able to establish that he'd had nothing whatsoever to do with any plot. His name was simply on a list of addresses given to the police. His solicitor, David Price, addressed the court.

'This was a stage-managed and nauseatingly self-congratulatory article, designed to boost the circulation of the *News of the World*. Imagine how it must have felt to spend nine months in Feltham Young Offenders Institution, accused of plotting to kidnap the UK's best known family, with the only "evidence" coming from a fraudster [Gashi] who was paid £10,000.'

Turcu won his case when the Screws finally admitted that he'd had nothing to do with the plot and that their front-page exclusive splash had been libellous.

Another of the plotters identified by the *News of the World* was Adrian Pasaraneu, a 27-year-old Romanian medical student. He didn't deny that he knew some of the other alleged plotters who were fellow countrymen. On one occasion, they had asked him to a party where he got into a speculative conversation with another guest who suggested that an easy way to make money would be to kidnap the Beckhams. Gashi or another of Mazher's operatives secretly recorded this casual conversation and passed it back to the paper. Pasaraneu was arrested with the others and subsequently incarcerated for 220 days, before being acquitted at the end of the abortive trial.

On his release, he was interviewed on BBC Radio 5 Live.

'I was fooled,' he said. 'I would have realised I was being set up if I was close to my co-defendants but there was no connection. They were people I'd met in England. I used to meet them once or twice a week to talk and play pool. I never realised the gravity of the situation. I think I'm entitled to some compensation.'

Three years later in March 2006, well into Coulson's tenure and his final *annus horribilis*, the paper was made to grovel again, this time by George Galloway, who demanded the sacking of star reporter Mazher Mahmood for an abortive sting he'd played. And the following month England footballer Wayne Rooney received £100,000 in damages from the News of the World and sister paper the Sun over articles falsely reporting that he'd slapped his fiancée, Coleen McLoughlin.

In June 2006, Rupert 'Digger' Murdoch had to dig into his coffers to pay around £100,000 in damages to Premiership footballer Ashley Cole after *Sun* reporters falsely suggested that he had been involved in a 'gay orgy'.

To spice up the year a little more, brash Scottish MP Tommy Sheridan was awarded £200,000 in libel damages against the *News of the World* over claims about his sexual activity. (The paper has since appealed, and police investigations have led to some of the witnesses in the trial being charged with perjury.)

This was swiftly followed in July 2006 by another major blow to the credibility of the *News of the World* and its editor when, after 2 weeks of deliberation, a jury at the Old Bailey cleared three alleged terrorists of plotting to buy 'red mercury', a radioactive material with which to construct a 'dirty' bomb.

Blame for the collapse of the three-month £1 million trial was laid squarely on the methods used by Mazher Mahmood, the *News of the World* reporter who'd first alerted Scotland Yard's anti-terrorist branch to what he claimed to have uncovered. It was one of many 'scoops' brought in by the burningly ambitious journalist for whom the impact of a story appears to be what counts above all else: nothing adds impact and authenticity to the front-page splash like bringing the police in. The story, which broke originally on September 26 2004 claimed:

"The *News of the World* has smashed a suspected terrorist plot to explode a dirty bomb on the streets of Britain."

The judicious inclusion of the word 'suspected' here may be seen as significant. The implication that there really had been a threat from radioactive bombs being detonated in public places in this country turned out to be completely unfounded, but Mahmood knew that a

story that frightened readers would have far more of the impact he sought. The report went on:
"In a joint operation with Scotland Yard, our reporter infiltrated a gang trying to buy radioactive material for a mystery Saudi Arabian – feared to be linked to al-Qaeda.'

Note the cynical use of the word 'feared', used once again to frighten the readers. The report ended,

'This guy has got a use for it over here – so we have to be very careful," our man was warned.'

Mahmood has frequently defended his stories and the methods by which he acquires them as being 'in the public interest', but some might find it hard to discern in this story a genuine sense in which his report and its sensationalist delivery could be interpreted as being 'in the public interest'. In this case, it turned out that the facts were so unthreatening as to be almost comical – a sort of whacky plot that Blackadder's Baldrick might have cooked up.

For a start, the deadly 'radioactive material' 'red mercury' is not just rare, as was claimed, but so rare that no scientific organisation has been able to confirm that it even exists. Some have suggested that 'red mercury' may be a fantasy material invented by Russian secret services to set up stings of their own; certainly to date no one has been able to produce a gram of the stuff, let alone the kilo for which Abdurahman Kanyare ('gang leader' from a 'sinister underground network') had suggested he had a customer who would pay $300,000.

Evidently, Somali wheeler-dealer Kanyare had heard of the stuff, not as an ingredient in bomb-making but as the Middle Eastern equivalent of Viagra – now a black market staple – with an additional application in washing so-called 'black dollars' – dollar bills that allegedly have been dyed black to disguise their value until such time as American Armed Forces in Africa need them. In fact, Kanyare seemed accustomed to dealing with a wide variety of obscure commodities, some more tangible than others – caviar from Poland, milk powder to Mozambique, fishing licences off the East African coast to Romanian trawlers. He was, in short, the kind of medium-scale black marketeer who will deal in anything if a buyer appears.

Kanyare told an associate, Roque Fernandes, a security guard at Coutts Bank, that he had been approached by a Saudi Arabian who had asked if he could supply some red mercury. Fernandes contacted Dominic Martins, a 45-year-old banker at Deutsche Bank who, in turn, contacted a man he knew in the chemical industry, referred to throughout by the *News of the World* as Mr B. Mr B contacted the News of the World with the information that someone was trying to buy this commodity in London. Whether he did this out of public-spiritedness or in the hope of financial gain has not been made clear.

Mazher Mahmood asked Mr B to set up a meeting between himself and Martins. There is a confusing account of the guise in which he presented himself as reported by the *News of the World* on September 26, 2004. On the one hand, we are told, he posed as a "Muslim extremist", and on the other as a potential supplier of the deadly chemical. The encounter was, apparently, successful and a further meeting was set up at Starbucks in Liverpool Street Station.

Mahmood thrillingly describes events: 'We infiltrated a sinister underworld network believed to be acting for a Mr Big from Saudi Arabia – a known *al-Qaeda hotbed*' (my italics). Further in the same report, he explains how he was taken to a series of meetings with members of a team hoping to supply the deadly material to the Saudi Mr Big, described as 'sympathetic to the Muslim cause' – whatever that means. Most Saudis, after all, are Muslim. Presumably this revelation, like the al-Qaeda hotbed, was used to make the coffee bar meeting sound more sinister. As is often the case in a *Screws* scare story, it's all in the telling – the rash of weasel words, vague and irrelevant, chosen to incite fear.

Mazher's blood was up; he had a story, all of his very own, which he'd taken a lot trouble putting together. The police were somehow persuaded that this was a genuine event, which presented a real and present threat to people in the streets of Britain, and specialist, armed anti-terrorist officers were brought in to arrest the three puzzled clowns, Kanyare, Martins and Fernandes.

But it didn't end there. The police chose to follow it up, and the three men were unjustly jailed on remand until their trial was scheduled in two years time (a fact which Andy Coulson overlooked in his valedictory rant about Clive Goodman's treatment.)

In hindsight the bare facts of the case are these: a buyer (Big, Saudi, pro-Muslim or otherwise) who never materialises, with money that is never produced, wants a substance that doesn't exist to do a job which doesn't exist, from a man who hadn't and never would have a gram of the stuff.

Did anyone else on the paper ask who these people were? What the stuff was really for? Where would it come from? Did it even exist? These were crucial, responsible questions that should have been asked before stark warnings of terror threats to the nation were issued.

When it came to it, the trial ended in the defendants' acquittal.

The cost of the investigation, the unjustified incarceration of the three defendants and the trial (which collapsed after three weeks) must have run to several million pounds of taxpayers' money. While it was admitted that the three conspirators had entered into discussions with a hazy view that there might be some money involved – commission, introduction fees, some percentage of the spend that was supposed to take place – there was an undeniable odour of fantasy about the whole event.

Why would a Saudi Arabian "Mr Big" choose to engage the services of an obscure Somalian wheeler-dealer? Who was he, anyway? The court never learned. The middlemen – opportunistic small-time hustlers, no doubt – had simply latched on to the possibility of turning a deal in a commodity which they didn't know didn't exist, although alleged to be highly radioactive and dangerous.

In a bizarre turn during this trial, Florim Gashi appeared as a key witness for the defence, when he told the court how he and Mahmood had concocted dozens of other stories over the years, most spectacularly the Beckham kidnap plot which had been trumpeted with such shameless gusto by Rebekah Wade.

Despite the obvious question marks hanging over Gashi's testimony – his conviction for dishonesty and an admission that he'd lied in a police statement about the kidnap case – his evidence was accepted at the Old Bailey. This in itself could have been a cock-up too far for Mazher, but somehow once again he managed to charm his bosses (Crone and Coulson) into supporting his continued presence in Wapping. When the whole absurd truth of the affair emerged, the paper's bosses defended themselves by saying that they truly believed there had been a genuine threat to life and limb on the streets of Britain, as they had told their readers. In the light of the quality of the evidence that emerged, it's surprising to a layman that Tom Crone, and those legal officers involved chose to proceed with the case at all.

It's surprising too, in both this case and the earlier Beckham kidnap fiasco, there was little criticism of either the police or the CPS for their willingness to cooperate with the *News of the World* on the basis of the insubstantial facts Mazher had produced. Why the police followed up on such minimal information raises worrying questions, though to be fair to the police, those who have met Mazher say he is dangerously plausible. As far as I'm aware, no commentators have yet tried to put a price on the time wasted by police on all of Mazher's activities, but accumulated over the years, that too must run to many millions.

Mazher's apparent plausibility was referred to by Stephen Solley QC, Martin's defence counsel, who accused Mazher of misleading the police, the CPS and the courts. He added that there was 'a huge danger of accepting Mr Mahmood's word in respect of any matter.' He also pointed out that the informant referred to as Mr B had deliberately misled the three men into agreeing to a deal which they would not have if they had known the truth. ' "B" created, through his activities with Mr Mahmood – who himself knew it was entirely a sham – a pincer movement so both their respective motives could be satisfied.' After the case was chucked out he added, 'This is a great tribute to the jury system and English justice and a dark day for the *News of the World.*'

But the pain this must have inflicted on Coulson and his staff was very effectively displaced by the drama that occurred the following month, which saw police crawling all over Wapping, arresting Clive Goodman and inquiry agent Glenn Mulcaire.

With all of this going on, Coulson picked the wrong moment to get into a spat with Max Clifford – one of his most important sources

– over 'Atomic Moggy', Kerry Katona. As a result of Max Clifford's freeze-out, Andy Coulson lost out on two stories he would have paid well for – Jude Law's affair with his children's nanny, and, more entertainingly, John Prescott's rumble in Admiralty Arch with Tracy Temple.

The continuing decline in the paper's sales may not be attributable to Coulson – almost every other national newspaper had shown a downturn as more alternative news sources have come online. Nevertheless, he must have found it hard to look Mr Murdoch in the eye knowing that the 4 million readership he'd inherited had dropped 15% to 3.4 million by the time he resigned over Clive Goodman's conviction in January 2007.

CHAPTER FIVE

A BIRMINGHAMBITION

There is no question that Mazher Mahmood has emerged as one of the most intriguing personalities in the recent history of the *News of the World*, indeed in British journalism. Our national press has seen the arrival of a significant number of successful, high-profile journalists from Asian backgrounds – a legacy of the strong journalistic traditions of the press in the subcontinent, which is widely served in English – and Mahmood is undoubtedly the most prominent of these. However, Mahmood is as industrious about obscuring himself as he is about revealing others, and among the hundreds of articles and profiles about him, very little about his personal life has been written. Some commentators even posit that his real name, age and origins have been deliberately falsified.

Extensive enquiries in his home town reveal that Mazher Mahmood, which is his real name, was born in his parents' modest, bow-windowed Victorian terrace house at 22 Floyer Road, in the Birmingham suburb of Small Heath on March 16, 1963. He was the second of two sons for Sultan and Shamim Mahmood, both journalists who had come from Pakistan to live in Britain in 1960 in the first major wave of immigration from the subcontinent.

Sultan was just 22 when he arrived, and his first priority was to look for work, anything to provide a home for himself and his young wife. Like many new arrivals from the subcontinent, he found a job as a conductor on a Birmingham bus, which kept the family afloat while he built up his journalistic and publishing activities. Within a few years he had founded and appointed himself Editor-in-Chief of Britain's first Urdu magazine, *Mashriq* (The East), a weekly digest of news from the subcontinent, with some local news and advertisements. As there was no Urdu language typesetting available the text had to be hand-written on screens for printing. The magazine circulated well into the '70s in those parts of Britain where significant Asian communities existed.

He also launched a monthly Urdu magazine for women, *Gharana* (Household), in which he was helped by his two young sons, Waseem and Mazher, who stapled the magazine together on the kitchen table and ran all over Birmingham distributing it to Asian grocery stores. Sultan was also a regular contributor to Birmingham's *Evening Mail*, freelanced for the *Daily Express* and served as UK bureau chief for the two biggest papers in Pakistan, the *Daily Nawaiwaqt* and the *Daily Nation*, a job which he held for over 20 years. As a result he was regarded as a significant figure within the Asian community. Although he didn't allow himself to get too involved in community politics, he was appointed a magistrate in 1977.

Sultan and his young family stayed in Floyer Road until the early '70s, when they moved to 72 Raddlebarn Road, Selly Park, in southwest Birmingham. This house, contained within a neat, late 19th-century red-brick terrace, wasn't much larger than the last, but it was in a distinctly better neighbourhood and out of the Asian ghetto that Small Heath was becoming. Selly Park was a nicely set-up middle-class area, well served with leafy open spaces. A few yards from the Mahmoods' house the steep wooded margins of the Worcester & Birmingham Canal provided an amenable play area. The boys went together to Raddlebarn Primary School, but split up when Waseem went on to Moseley Grammar, *alma mater* of such varied notables as Jasper Carrot, Gladstone Small, and first black Tory MP John (now Lord) Taylor, as well as Bev Bevan and Richard Tandy of The Move and ELO.

Mazher went to King Edward VI Five Ways, a top Birmingham

grammar school that also produced ex-BBC Chief Michael Checkland, Tom Butler, Bishop of Southwark and former Rugby international Keith Fielding. Leaving after the 5th form, the young Mazher made no lasting impression on those who taught him, although like his older brother he achieved a satisfactory crop of good grade O-levels. He was also a competent cricketer, and on Sunday mornings, after sessions learning the Koran, he would go off with Waseem to play for their mosque's cricket team. On one occasion, in a match against a Walsall mosque, Mazher decided that the umpire (an imam) was cheating. In an early demonstration of his confrontational personality, Mazher led his side off the pitch.

The Mahmood boys joined up again for their A-levels at Sutton Coldfield College, Waseem to do drama, Mazher to do economics, English and sociology. While Waseem continued his drama studies in Worcester, Mazher went down to Middlesex Poly to pursue a degree in humanities. Once he'd arrived at the Poly, Mazher found it impossible to settle down in the student routine and was frustrated from the start, wanting desperately to get on with something – anything. He even briefly considered joining Pakistan Airlines, simply to get out into the real world. In the end, neither of the brothers lasted longer than a year in tertiary education.

The roots of Mazher's hard-driving ambition aren't clear, but that he and his brother went on to succeed in their fields well beyond the average expectations of Birmingham Asians is not too surprising, given their father's background. In addition, the family were not especially devout Muslims, and by their late teens both boys, although still observing the Fast, no longer engaged in the ritual of five-times-daily prayer, which allowed them greater flexibility in pursuing targets. At 21, Waseem joined the BBC as a producer in the Asian Programmes Unit at the Pebble Mill studios in Birmingham, and Mazher, too, decided that it was time for him to become a journalist.

It was probably Mazher's constant contact as a child with journalism in the raw that planted the seed of his fascination with newspapers and investigative reporting. He may have recognised at an early age the adrenalin-pumping buzz in finding hard, fresh news before anyone else; the romance, the danger, the risk and subterfuge involved in finding stories that would shock and amaze; the thrill of knowing that as a result of your own observation, analysis and skills at extracting intelligence, you would be the first to tell a waiting world. He'd always been impressed by the power of journalism and by the influence held by his father – though he was more well-respected commentator than investigative reporter. While Mazher was at the Poly, an Asian diplomat was murdered in Leicester, and Mazher went there and researched the event himself. At the same time, he nurtured contacts among the fomenting community in Handsworth. Since he'd been at school, he'd hung around the offices of the *Birmingham Post*, trying to persuade them to give him some kind of work or apprenticeship, and he was bitterly disappointed when he failed ever to get a traineeship there.

In the meantime, Waseem, who had been working in Bombay, managed to get his younger sibling a job as UK correspondent to a Bollywood movie magazine called *Super*, where he filed British Asian movie news and gossip. At *Super* Mazher had his first experience producing a full-scale national story by exploiting events that had fallen into his lap, and he did so in a manner which was a clear indication of his future ethos.

Some close friends came round to dinner one evening at the family home in Selly Park. Although Sultan himself would not have considered participating in the kind of business activities in which these friends were engaged, it wasn't his place to judge and, although not direct kin, these friends had complete trust in the Mahmood family. Over the meal, they described, quite openly in the privacy of the Mahmoods' home, a video piracy operation they had set up. At the time, there was no formal, legitimate distribution of Asian videos and in a sense they could be said to have been providing a service. They were young and pleased with themselves, boasting how they had managed to "borrow" a print of a new Bollywood movie from an airport warehouse for four hours – just long enough to copy it and return it before it was missed.

Young Mazher's eagerness for a scoop would not allow him to resist exploiting what was obviously a good, saleable story – the kind of exposé of insidious crime that the big tabloids loved. Within days after the dinner, he began touting the story around the British papers but was told it was too 'ethnic' a story. Disappointed but undeterred, he sold the story to *Super* instead. He did a comprehensive hatchet job on his family's friends, naming them and their address. He even took a photograph of their house, which *Super* blithely and somewhat naively published. When the story broke, Mazher's betrayal caused great furore in the Asian community. The incident was also picked up by British media and landed him on his local TV news (then presented by Ann Robinson). It was, by any journalistic standards, a disgraceful act of betrayal. Mazher's parents were dumfounded by his utter disregard for their family's strong, traditional rules of friendship.

'My parents were mad,' Mazher admitted in a rare interview (for Andrew Marr's book, *My Trade*). 'They threatened to throw me out for exposing family friends, and it did take a long time to get back with them.' It says something for Mazher's powers of persuasion that he managed to talk himself back into their favour at all.

As a result of the Video Piracy exposé's success (as a news story, if not as a way to win friends), Mazher felt confident enough to present himself with his cuttings from *Super* at the offices of *The People*, where he met Laurie Manifold, the justifiably revered mentor of young investigative hacks. Mazher was under 20, but the editors immediately recognized his talents. In addition, they were not unconscious of the benefits of having an Asian on the ground when Asians were still rare in mainstream British journalism. They took him on eagerly and he set to work on stories of child labour rackets in London and other race-related abuses, learning quickly under Manifold and developing a formidable base on which to build his own journalistic techniques. He spent much of his time doing what he enjoyed most – unmasking 'vice' scams. Colleagues working with him at the time recall that he particularly liked to keep copies of all the photos that had been taken, whether real or, as often happened (and still happens) posed by his more voluptuous undercover colleagues.

More heavyweight opportunities came his way when race riots erupted in the early '80s. Using his ethnicity and longstanding contacts in Handsworth, Birmingham – an epicentre of the troubles – he was able to get close in among the communities who were causing disruption, and join them while they threw bottles. It was then, in

1985, that Robin Morgan at *The Sunday Times* took him on to cover the riots and to investigate tensions within the Sikh community. At *The Sunday Times* he also did notable work on the Paedophile Information Exchange, several immigration rackets. Again, making good use of his ethnicity, he uncovered a Libyan hit squad training at Abingdon Flying School.

But at 25, he was showing signs of a tendency to bend the facts and edit interviews to match the story he wanted to tell. On May 8, 1988, *The Sunday Times* published a story with Mazher's by-line about Edward Pease-Watkin, headmaster of Packwood Haugh, a highly regarded Shropshire prep school. David Todd, an embittered teacher who had been dismissed from the school, was looking for revenge and had contacted the paper. Mazher was assigned. With very selective use of what he'd been told by other staff and pupils, Mahmood wrote a vicious, damning piece, painting as bleak a picture of the headmaster as he could, adding that the headmaster was currently the subject of a police investigation (in truth, based only upon Todd's allegations). The following week saw an uproar with indignant letters to the paper, all supporting the headmaster – an outstanding if somewhat old-fashioned teacher who had brought the school up from 70 pupils to 300 in his 30-years tenure. The police responded that they had completed their investigations before the article was published and had found no evidence to support Todd's allegations.

It was also at *The Sunday Times* that Mazher showed for a second time his remarkable ruthlessness when it comes to getting a hot story. By this time, the Mahmoods had moved from Raddlebarn Road to Greenland Road, a short walk up the Pershore Road to the Pebble Mill studios where Waseem worked. The elder brother was doing well at BBC Television, and Pebble Mill was in its heyday, with a cornerstone current affairs programme and a string of BAFTA awards to its name.

One night over dinner, Waseem casually mentioned to his family that there was a significant amount of moonlighting going on among full-time staff at Pebble Mill. Staff were using BBC equipment and resources in their own time to make programmes for outside competing companies – strictly against BBC rules. Mazher lifted his head sharply, smelling blood – employees of an august public organisation cheating the licence-payers. There was always a market for stories like that.

Telling them that he was putting together a programme for Channel 4, Mahzer began ringing the people involved, many of whom he knew from his years hanging around the bar in Pebble Mill bar with his brother. They took his calls and discussed his requirements with him, as a friend. When Mazher had filled his dossier, he wrote a full, damning report in *The Sunday Times*, attributing it to an unnamed 'BBC source'. Waseem was horrified when he was inevitably identified as that source.

'Private family chatter around the kitchen table had been regurgitated in a sensational story,' Waseem said afterwards. 'I protested that I knew nothing about it, but it was hopeless, and I had no choice but to resign.'

The incident curtailed forever both Waseem's career at the BBC and his relationship with his brother. During the course of a two-hour interview with Waseem, a charming and cultivated man, it was clear that he still feels bitter over his brother's utter callousness. Waseem writes about the incident in his recently published book, Good Morning Afghanistan, in which he chronicles the process of setting up a unifying radio station in a nation coming out of a long, ugly civil war.

In a flashback he recalls what happened after he had to leave the BBC...

Professionally I found myself banished to that barren wilderness which was 'disgraced ex-BBC' from which very few ever returned. Suddenly, all the awards and all the successes meant nothing and overnight I had become an unemployable pariah who had allegedly sold out his friends to the vultures of popular journalism.

While my brother's career shot into the stratosphere, fuelled by his amazing exposé of wrongdoing at the BBC, mine spiralled equally spectacularly downwards towards the gutter. Friends who had been dangling lucrative contracts in front of me while I was still at the Beeb now stopped taking my calls. Even their secretaries who had been on first name terms with me suddenly began denying that they even knew me. Media, for all its rivalries, remained very much a closed shop where everyone looked out for each other, and before long I realised that my chances of gaining employment in the British media again were rather bleak. In the eyes of my peers and contemporaries I had committed the most heinous sin, and my humiliation was complete when I couldn't even get a lowly job at my local radio station.

Some ghosts become impossible to exorcise, and my brother's betrayal was one of them. It taunted me every single moment and I knew that it would continue to do so until my dying day. There were, and still are times when the anger is overwhelming and while I try very hard to forgive him, I find it nigh on impossible to forget what he did. The one question that haunts me to this day is 'Why?'

Not surprisingly, the two brothers have barely spoken since, although Mazher again successfully used his powers of persuasion to stay on good terms with his parents, despite his unequivocal display of disloyalty.

However, Mazher's arrogance did catch up with him at *The Sunday Times*, where he was caught red-handed in a manner that permanently tainted him in the eyes of a number of colleagues, especially those in the more serious papers. Roy Greenslade, managing editor at *The Sunday Time*s in 1988, recalls the incident well. Mazher had filed a police story based largely on an agency report, upon which he had built. The published version contained an error of fact; this was identified and pointed out to him. Normally, for a comparatively minor mistake like this, the maximum punishment would have been no more than a verbal warning. He hadn't made any other errors up until then and his editors were generally happy with what he'd achieved.

Instead of admitting to his mistake, Mazher insisted that the error had emanated from the original agency report. Greenslade contacted the agency, who forwarded to him a replica of the report – which contained no such error. Nevertheless, Mazher persisted in proclaiming his innocence. As everything was logged in the main computer, it was an easy matter to check the original. Roy asked the man who was responsible for the operating of the computer room to find it for him. Fifteen minutes later he arrived in Roy Greenslade's office looking shocked and closed the door behind him. He told Greenslade that he'd been to the computer room to ask for what he wanted when one of the computer operators said something that brought him up short.

'That's funny – a reporter was in last week asking for the same report and we found he'd gone and sat down and was trying to change it on the computer; we had to chuck him out.' The reporter was Mazher Mahmood.

Precisely to avoid this sort of abuse, journalists are forbidden to enter the mainframe; the operator was in trouble for admitting Mazher in the first place and for then not reporting the incident. But more brazen was the fact that Mazher had been in there, shamelessly attempting to tamper with the evidence of his misdemeanour – a cardinal sin in serious journalism. Greenslade was astonished that a reporter should have gone to such lengths to avoid a verbal bollocking for the original misdemeanour. Within the context of *The Sunday Times*, it was fairly shocking behaviour that could not be tolerated.

Roy Greenslade spoke to news editor Michael Williams, who was a great supporter of Mazher's, as a result of which the computer room boss went off to produce a report, which Greenslade then took to the Editor, Andrew Neill. The subsequent meeting to discuss this serious breach of security was attended by the Greenslade, Williams and Neill, as well as the deputy editor, Ivan Fallon (now CEO of Independent Newspapers).

When the facts had been read out, Andrew Neill looked aghast. This kind of underhand treatment of the truth was absolutely at odds with the traditional journalistic standards that he championed at *The Sunday Times*.

He looked around at his three colleagues. 'Recommendations?'

Greenslade proposed dismissal.

Michael Williams agreed.

Ivan Fallon proposed instant dismissal.

But Andrew Neill pointed out that it would be unnecessarily

harsh to sack him in the week before Christmas, even if Mazher wasn't known to be a Christian, and that it should be delayed until after the holiday. They considered this for a few moments, until Michael Williams insisted that it was absurd to pussyfoot around and it needed to be done straight away. The others agreed and emerged from Neill's office to put their decision into action.

Michael Williams found on his desk a letter from Mazher Mahmood resigning from the paper. He had already left and was never seen again at *The Sunday Times*. At no point since, when Roy Greenslade has several times publicly recounted the incident, has Mahmood ever attempted to dispute his version of events.

Having jumped ship at *The Sunday Times* before he was pushed, Mazher managed to get a production job at TVAM for Sir David Frost. It didn't last long. He soon got bored working within the necessarily tight disciplines of television current affairs and recognised that his talents lay in the far more immediate and individually focused medium of newspapers. Using his existing contacts at the *News of the World*, at the age of 26, he moved into the Wapping newsroom in 1991.

Once Mazher was reinstalled at Fortress Wapping, it became obvious that the *News of the World* was his natural habitat. Here was an atmosphere where impact was king and unhelpful facts were not allowed to spoil a good story. It was the start of a relationship that has lasted over 16 years. He possessed great skill – on the phone, wheedling, gently winkling information from people – and face-to-face, he had a powerful charm. With his good looks and style, Mazher was well served by his air of a successful young Asian businessman.

In his early years at the *News of the World*, Mazher worked more or less conventionally, as he had done at *The Sunday Times*, targeting genuine wrongdoers who deserved to be unmasked and brought to justice – the human traffickers, the paedophiles, bent policemen and corrupt council officials. But it was the sensational story of a high-profile celebrity that he sought most, not because the injustice he was revealing was any greater, but because he recognised the growing public appetite for salacious, prurient insights into the lives of the famous. Mazher was learning that it was celebrity-based stories, more than anything else, that could consistently deliver him the front-page splashes he craved. As the '90s lurched forward, he scored several big scoops in between regular revelations about cops, strippers and lustful vicars.

It was Mazher who made much of David Mellor's affair with actress Antonia de Sancha, a story which caught the public imagination because the MP had none of the obvious characteristics of an active Lothario and which gave birth to the appealing and indestructible myth that Mellor had insisted on making love to the actress in his Chelsea football strip – a claim vehemently denied by Mellor ever since, to no avail. Mellor would in any case have been a cherished scalp for any tabloid editor, since a few years earlier, when several had published pictures of dead football fans at Hillsborough, he'd got to his feet in the House of Commons and told the tabloid press they were 'drinking at the last chance saloon.'

Regrettably, to a muted accompaniment of the gnashing of toothless gums by the Parliamentary Committee for Media Culture and Sport and the PCC, Mazher and his Wapping colleagues have had many, many more last chances to drink over the years since – especially as Mazher perfected his own unique *modus operandi*, inventing the undercover persona who was to become notorious as the *"Fake Sheikh"*.

CHAPTER SIX

A FEIKH OF ARABY

With his invention of the Fake Sheikh, Mazher Mahmood changed the course of his life irreversibly: the role elevated him from being just another *News of the World* hack into a mythical figure, almost as famous as the paper itself. There has been wide speculation about details of both the 'Sheikh' and the man. Although always very chary of revealing anything about himself, after one of the 'Sheikh's' best known and most spectacular performances (with Sophie, Countess of Wessex), Mazher was willing to reveal some of his methods to a *News of the World* reporter.

'The tools of my trade are a wardrobe of over a dozen *djellabia* (loose-fitting, full-length Arab robes). Many of them are traditional white, though a few are for evening wear,' he told Sarah Arnold. 'Normally I wear the white robe, called an *agal*, with a variety of head scarves and Arab rings, called the *ghatra*. I also have a black, gold-embroidered robe to wear on top. This would only be worn by royalty in the Middle East.

'But what makes it all work is the entourage. I have a whole team of people including my two stand-in sheikhs, accompanied by security staff, assistants and Arab women covered by traditional dress.

'Every whim of the Sheikh is catered for... his glass is always full of apple juice because the Sheikh is teetotal. And when he clicks his fingers one of the assistants produces a cigar which is then lit for him.

'The robes and entourage are so convincing that other Arabs staying at the hotels often come up and shake hands, which adds even more to the image.'

Key to the success of a Fake Sheikh sting was identifying a target's greed, commercial ambition or financial straits and presenting himself as a bottomless source of money, which always put Mahzer in a disarmingly strong position with all but the most righteous. Although he has had failures, the large majority of his victims have been completely taken in thanks in large part to a dedicated team which has become increasingly slick and efficient with experience.

Mahmood's investigations unit has been supported by the *News of the World* with an exceptional budget, rumoured to run to £500,000 a year, which has allowed him to hire whatever trappings are required to create total verisimilitude in his deceptions – suites in The Dorchester, Rolls Royces and Ferraris, lavishly clothed fake harems to accompany him. At times he has employed a team of up to 12 assistants and back-ups. In addition to a permanent bodyguard, he has often been assisted by an old friend, Dr Akbar Ali Malik, a practising lawyer since 1980.

Malik also holds an MA in history, political science and Urdu, an MSc in Refugee Studies from the University of East London and a doctorate in Jurisprudence. He has written four books on Islamic Law and British Immigration Law and is currently CEO of the Malik Law Chamber, a small firm based at 233 Bethnal Green Road, East London, which describes itself as 'the country's leading specialists on immigration law'. Malik first came into contact with Mazher Mahmood when he started selling stories to him in the late '80s and early '90s. Despite Mazher's reputed general reluctance to bond, he and Malik got on well, and he was impressed with the legal help Malik was able to offer, particularly when it came to stories uncovering immigration scams.

But once he was appointed Investigations Editor in 1995, Mazher started to focus less on solid, broadly creditable exposés and more on celebrity stings, which his editor, Phil Hall, would often splash on the front page. For these, Mazher began orchestrating the deceptions for which he is now famous, and, from time to time, Malik was invited to join the Fake Sheikh's entourage.

In August 1997, Malik was part of the team that entrapped John Alford, the popular young actor who played fire-fighter Billy Ray in the hit TV show "London's Burning". Mazher, posing as 'Sheikh Mohammed al Kareem', approached Alford with the offer of £100,000 to open a nightclub in Dubai. In the course of discussions the team successfully duped Alford into offering to get some drugs for them. The actor was video-recorded discussing the deal (and even bowing to the 'Sheikh'). Mazher claimed their investigation showed Alford was a drugs dealer and the tape was handed over to the police. As a result he was charged, and at Snaresbrook Crown Court he admitted supplying a Class A drug – although, he said in mitigation, only as a result of being pressured to do so by *News of the World* journalists. Along with other members of Mazher's team, Ali Malik gave evidence at Alford's trial, where he described himself a 'freelance journalist and lawyer'. Malik even asked the court that the name of his legal practice not be mentioned in open court, to which the judge agreed during legal argument in the absence of the jury. Ultimately, little account was taken of Mazher's encouraging him to commit the crime, and Alford was jailed for supplying cannabis and cocaine. As a direct result, his career was destroyed. He has since reverted to his real name of John Fallon and dropped totally out of sight.

After the Alford sting, Malik became a regular freelancer for the *News of the World*'s investigations unit. He was involved in the entrapment of the Earl of Hardwicke in 1999, and, in 2001, Malik himself played the Fake Sheikh for the Countess of Wessex sting, while Mazher played his urbane, westernised sidekick.

When Mazher's team tried – and failed dismally – to suborn George Galloway in 2006, Galloway found in his own subsequent inquiries that one of the Fake Sheikh's false companies was registered at Malik's Bethnal Green office.

Malik has shown that he can be extremely litigious when the media question his reputation. In November 1999, he reported the *Sunday People* to the Press Complaints Commission for harassment and the wrongful use of subterfuge. He claimed an undercover reporter had visited the offices under false pretences and a photographer had taken pictures of his staff. The PCC dismissed the complaint and strongly rebuked Malik for wasting its time, but when in February 2006, *The Sunday Times* ran a story alleging that Malik offered an undercover reporter at the paper advice on how immigrants could get British citizenship if they entered into gay marriages, Malik immediately instructed a leading firm of libel lawyers to sue the paper.

Malik won, and *The Sunday Times* was forced to print an apology and cough up £20,000 in damages on July 18, 2006. For several years, one of Mazher's most experienced in-house colleagues was Scotsman Gerry Brown. One of the great investigative journalists of his day, Brown earned the nation's gratitude by reeling in the slippery and mendacious Jeffrey Archer over his brief encounter with prostitute Monica Coghlan. Before dying in January 2004 at age 60, Gerry Brown had set up a company specialising in surveillance equipment. He and Mazher, both of them tough and uncompromising, made a formidable partnership, and Gerry Brown entered whole-heartedly into the spirit of the game. It was he who played one of the 'Sheikh's' minders when the paper exposed Newcastle United bosses Freddie Shepherd and Dougie Hall in a Spanish brothel.

Gerry Brown's son Conrad became Mazher's surveillance chief, photographer and camera operator, responsible for covert recordings or filming of Mazher's setups. (He also played the Sheikh's lackey in the infamous Sophie Wessex sting.) Cameras would be installed in strategically positioned shirt buttons, Filofaxes and briefcases and used to vivid effect. As recently as November 2007, former bra model Sophie Anderton was filmed snorting coke and stripping off to deliver sex for £10,000 (for all to see, now that the *News of the World* offers soft pornography on its family website).

People working in the *Screws* newsroom say that members of Mazher's team were always committed, notoriously secretive and loyal to him. Often playing roles as various members of the 'Sheikh's' entourage, an integral component of the deception, they painstakingly planned their campaigns, preparing the scene with lavish attention to detail. Names would be invented and checked for comebacks, bogus companies set up and West End offices rented as required. Elaborate websites would be created to add credibility to the organisation the 'Sheikh' was purporting to represent. Pay-as-you-go mobiles were used to avoid anyone being traced back to the *News of the World*. People on the inside say that stings have cost up to £40,000 to set up, and generally, in terms of front-page splashes if not the preservation of truth, they've paid off.

Mazher plays the 'Sheikh' with great theatricality. Once contact is established – often in several stages, both to belay suspicion and sharpen the target's appetite – the target is invited to meet the 'Sheikh'. Upon arrival at the door of a lavish (sometimes £3,000 a night) suite, he is given a systematic frisking before being allowed to enter. The target would be told of the 'Sheikh's' likes and dislikes – all part of a pantomime to leave them in no doubt that they were about to enter the presence of an extremely powerful man, thus encouraged to focus on him and dispel any lurking suspicions. He is then ushered in with great ceremony to find the 'Sheikh' lolling on an enormous cushion, puffing away on a hookah, usually with his supposedly favourite cherry tobacco glowing in the pipe's bowl. By the time the Sheikh limply shakes hands with his mark and gazes at him with hooded brown eyes, the deception is usually complete.

A former colleague describing members of Mazher's team says, 'Seeing people being taken in by their performance gives them a tremendous feeling of power and achievement.'

Mahmood likes to play his team in different formations, bringing on extra players when appropriate. The part he plays himself in the charades also varies; in a few he hasn't appeared at all – especially now that his face can be seen in his entry on Wikipedia. One of the consistently key players is the 'roper', who makes initial contact with the victim. He must be completely plausible, well turned out and very fluent in English. The approach almost invariably contains an offer of money – either as an investment, for a purchase or, in a couple of instances, as political funding.

Once the roper has won the confidence of the victim, he suggests that the victim meet his boss, who is usually played by Mazher. A well-rehearsed scene, or perhaps two or three over a few days to add authenticity, will be acted out by Mazher's cast with their target. Depending on the nature of the sting, the team, often without Mazher himself at first, will initially set out to convince the target that he is on the verge of receiving a large and unexpected sum of money. Then, through a cross-talk in which few direct questions are asked, the team will try to trick him into either admitting to using drugs (sometimes by asking him to procure some for them), or uttering spontaneous, damning indiscretions about other public figures, especially royalty. Of course the tactic doesn't always work, for example: Mazher's team stalked Carole Caplin for several weeks before gleaning anything worth publishing. In the end they got no more than a few indiscreet comments about people she'd met through her friend, Cherie Blair.

Generally, once the team has extracted all it can from a sting and the story is about to go to press, the paper calls the target's agent on a Friday night or Saturday morning to inform him that a story is going to appear in the *News of the World* on Sunday and to get a reaction from the target. This is a legal safeguard as much as anything else, as it gives the unfortunate individual who is about to be splashed all over the paper a 'right of reply' – although there's seldom time to organise a useful response. For the target, the initial revelation that he is going to be in the paper at all is bad enough – it's never going to be anything positive – but the 24 hours of waiting to see how the paper has spun the story must be excruciating.

Mazher's team of players changes as he meets people of differing skills and characteristics. There is a pleasing irony to the recruitment of Sri Lankan Kishan Athulathmudali. Kishan possesses a thoroughly upper-crust English accent and manner; he is intelligent, personable and very articulate as well. In 1999 he joined R-JH Public Relations, a company run by Murray Harkin and Sophie, Countess of Wessex. As an account manager with the firm, he worked closely with the Countess in organising her trips abroad. But after two years, he fell out with his bosses over his approach to the job. Still employed by them but feeling disgruntled and vengeful, in early March 2001 he trotted round the corner to Brooks Mews to see Max Clifford to whom he alleged that Murray Harkin engaged in dodgy practices and that Sophie used her royal connections to curry business.

Max swiftly sold the story to Rebekah Wade at the *News of the World* and introduced Kishan to the paper, where he entered into extensive talks and quickly found a rapport, especially with Mazher. The two decided that this was a job for the Fake Sheikh and made plans for Mazher's team to go undercover to catch out the Countess and Harkin in any way they could. Towards the end of March 2001, R-JH found out that Kishan had joined forces with the paper, and, becoming suspicious, took out an injunction against him. However the legal move came too late, as the News of the World ultimately didn't need to use any of Kishan's allegations. As it turned out, Kishan's and Mazher's plan had given rise to a classic Fake Sheikh sting, and the poor woman walked straight into it, arms akimbo.

Soon after Mazher had been given the lead by Kishan, he rang R-JH PR and asked to speak to Murray Harkin, the Countess of Wessex's business partner. He explained, as senior assistant to a Sheikh Mohamed, that his company was setting up a major leisure complex in Dubai, and they wished to promote it in the Gulf as well as raise their company's profile in the UK, where they were intending to expand. He wanted to meet to discuss the possibility of R-JH acting for them in this. Harkin hastily agreed to meet the Sheikh and his entourage the following day. In a room at the Park Lane Hilton, Harkin introduced himself to a pair of be-robed individuals, 'Sheikh Mohamed' (played by Ali Malik), sucking perfunctorily on his hookah, and his suave, fluent English-speaking assistant (played by Mazher Mahmood), wafting solicitously behind.

They both shook hands with Harkin, who found himself making involuntarily obeisance at such apparently wealthy potential punters. The assistant described in more detail what they were planning and what they wanted R-JH to do for them: specifically, he wanted to know if Prince Edward would be with Sophie when she came over for launch parties. Harkin, having done nothing to check the bona fides of the Arab plutocrats, believed he was firmly on the trail of a hot new client and hurled whatever caution he might have brought with him to the wind whistling down Park Lane and started talking.

He told them that Prince Edward had very recently been on a trip to Dubai when his wife was promoting a client. 'So, it's like she's bought into it, and she got Edward involved and bought into it as well.' Harkin also explained ways in which they could get around the ban on using photographs of royal personages to directly promote a product, adding carelessly, 'and anyway, you can buy photographs of her meeting the Queen or meeting various people and you can do whatever you like with those, so, in that sense you get endorsement from it.'

Mazher, applying his patient, softlee softlee approach, arranged a second meeting with Harkin alone, to be held at the Dorchester. At this meeting, Harkin boasted that if they dressed up a launch party as a charity event, Sophie could get Sean Connery to come along, and Julia Roberts too, on the grounds that as an American she wouldn't turn down an invitation from an English princess. He reassured them that once Sophie was committed, she'd deliver as much as they could wish for, in PR terms, especially at gigs abroad where she was less restricted.

By this time, Harkin was so sure of the deal, he encouraged Sophie to come to a third meeting over lunch, again at the Dorchester. Sophie didn't take much persuading. She sent her police bodyguard over to the Dorchester to pick up a menu so she could plan her lunch, and turned up on the appointed day with Harkin, Brett Perkins (an R-JH account executive), and her police guard, Inspector Tim Nash, who posted himself outside the door of the suite. There to greet them were the 'Sheikh' and his suave assistant, both dressed in Western suits, another 'Arab' and an English gofer (played by Conrad Brown), and the final leg of the sting was on.

Once he'd got the young Countess talking, even Mazher must have found it hard to contain his glee as she spouted a torrent of indiscretion. The 'Sheikh' asked casually what she thought about her brother-in-law, Prince Charles, and Camilla Parker-Bowles, and how being divorced might affect his becoming King. Instead of discreetly declining to offer her views in the prescribed royal way, she explained with all the benefit of inside knowledge to a complete stranger that Charles and Camilla would marry, but only after the Queen Mother had died. Thus she made the unknown 'Sheikh' privy to significant information about the Royal Family to which the British people were not.

She went on to claim, apparently quite seriously, that the public had put her 'on the plinth vacated by Diana,' but she wouldn't be playing the part as 'vigorously'. She described Tony Blair as 'too presidential' and his wife Cherie as 'absolutely horrid'. She thought Gordon Brown's budget was 'pap', designed merely to win votes. William Hague, she opined, had a funny-shaped mouth, spoke oddly and wouldn't win the forthcoming election. John Major she described as wooden and a bit of a has-been, although she could still get him along to a function any time, if required.

All this, and a bagful more of indiscretions, were pure gold to Mazher, and after she'd gone, he was offered even more muck by Harkin, who had remained behind, no doubt eager to close the deal. The 'Arabs' quizzed him on rumours about Prince Edward's sexuality, to which he replied, 'There have been rumours for years about Edward. I'm a great believer that there's no smoke without fire.' He blithely chatted on about how it was possible to buy 'testers' of cocaine in Holland, and offered the opinion that it was 'crazy' that cannabis was still illegal in Britain. He also admitted that he liked 'to do the odd line of coke' but finding the stuff was 'like, a nightmare!' He also suggested that if required he could arrange suitable guests at a party to launch the Dubai leisure complex in Britain; he could get A-list celebrities, and nice compliant 'boys – all good jobs!'

After he'd finally ushered Harkin from the suite, Mazher must have jumped for joy as he raced for his laptop to hammer it all out, before phoning the R-JH offices to explain how they'd just been well and truly stung.

This launched a whirlwind of damage-limitation exercise on the part of the royal press staff. Buckingham Palace officials contacted the Press Complaints Commission, on the grounds that the PCC code is clear: Subterfuge can only be used when acting in the public interest. The *News of the World* could, possibly, have argued that checking whether or not the countess was using her royal title to assist her business was in the public interest, and if they were unable to prove that, they would drop the story.

But by this stage, Director of Communications at the Palace, Simon Walker had offered editor Rebekah Wade a compromise – an exclusive, on-the-record interview with the countess in exchange for all of the recordings of her and her partner's indiscretions. (The PCC denied being involved in this deal, though several commentators have pointed out that the chief executive of the PCC, Guy Black shared a flat with Mark Bolland, Prince Charles's principal private secretary).

On April Fool's Day, what the readers of the *News of the World* got – in itself pretty spectacular – was an in-depth, unrestricted interview with the Countess of Wessex, conducted in the Regency Drawing-room of Buckingham Palace by experienced *Screws* hack, Carole Aye Maung. The resulting five-page piece was extraordinary in its total frankness, and generally shed a benign light on Sophie. It addressed head-on such thorny issues as Prince Edward's sexuality (straight), her own lack of child-bearing (just wait) and the public's unfavourable comparisons between her and the late Princess Diana (too bad).

What the readers weren't told is that as Ms Aye Maung and her photographer arrived at the Palace, audiotapes of the Countess's discussion with Mazher Mahmood that had taken place two weeks before were being delivered into the safe custody of Farrer & Co, the Queen's solicitors. It was, in short, a trade off – an unprecedented, on-the-record interview had been granted in exchange for a set of tapes which contained pure dynamite, in the deal brokered between *News of the World* and the Palace.

It was to be expected that while the tapes themselves had left Wapping, the transcript of what they contained was still safely tucked away at the News International premises, to be systematically leaked during the week that followed, so that by the end of it, most of the contents were in the public domain, and the *News of the World* had a strong case for running the piece themselves – another masterstroke from Mr Tom Crone – and Rebekah had two massive splashes, two weeks running – the result of adroit manipulation of the unfortunate Countess.

In any event, in what looked like an open-and-shut case of entrapment, the regulatory body of the national press had nothing to say about the entrapment of a member of the Royal Family by a major national newspaper. In the *Independent*, commentator David Lister put it succinctly.

'The Countess of Wessex may have been both naive and foolish;

she certainly seems to have divulged personal matters to a complete stranger with indecent haste in a quest for a business deal. But she is not a criminal, a drug taker or a philanderer. And using entrapment on a completely innocent person in the hope of a few verbal indiscretions gives a depressing signal about the *News of the World*'s evolving attitude to investigative reporting; it should alarm people far beyond the House of Windsor.'

Back at Wapping, Mazher Mahmood was so impressed by the part Kishan had played in setting up the whole scam that he offered him a full-time job on his investigations team. Kishan's main function now is to act as Mazher's 'roper', going out to make the first contact and convincing the target of the Fake Sheikh's bona fides, which he is reported to do with great subtlety, even making fun of the 'Sheikh' behind his back, and when conversations with the target begin, apologising for the 'Sheikh's' inquisitive nature, in a variation on the good cop/bad cop routine. Over the last few years, Kishan has become a key member of Mazher's team and is today his No 2. They are now the only two permanent members of *News of the World* staff on the investigations unit.

The full line-up of people fooled by the *djellabias* and hookah pipe is long and sometimes extraordinary.

Newcastle United bosses Freddie Shepherd and Doug Hall, recorded slagging off their clubs fans, describing Geordie women as 'dogs' and referring to their star player, Alan Shearer as 'Mary Poppins', all the while ensconced with Mazher and Gerry Brown on a binge in a Spanish brothel.

Sven Goran Eriksson, entrapped during a trip to Dubai, when Kishan (as the roper) enticed the former England football coach into making disparaging remarks about the England football team and revealing that he was entering into negotiations to become the manager of Aston Villa FC.

Blue Peter presenter Richard Bacon, who was sacked by the BBC in 1998 after the *News of the World* extracted an admission from him that he'd used cocaine.

Joe Yorke, 10th Earl of Hardwicke, one of Mazher's more innocent victims, is an unassuming man. An English earl without any great inherited wealth, he is in most respects a normal citizen and was trying to keep together a small scooter business he operated in South London. He wasn't a big society figure and generally kept a low profile. He was not an active member of the House of Lords, nor was he in any other way a public figure whose actions might be considered to be in the public interest. The only reason Mazher targeted him was because he possessed a title.

In 1999, Mazher and his team showed up at his premises and announced to Hardwicke and his business partner, Stephan Thwaites, that they wanted to buy £100,000 worth of scooters. It was like manna from heaven to the beleaguered company, and terms were quickly agreed. However, before the contract was signed and sealed, Mazher invited the partners for an expensive evening at the Savoy. There he kept the drink flowing and moved the conversation onto the topic of cocaine. Mazher asked if Joe could get some for him – a ploy he's used dozens of times – and waited for the unsuspecting man to stumble into his unsubtle trap.

The scooter deal hadn't been signed, and it was more or less vital to Hardwicke's business. His priority was to keep his customer sweet. If the rich Arab wanted cocaine, then he'd get some for him. Hardwicke knew a few people who used it regularly and it didn't take him long to track down a supplier.

When the stuff arrived in their private room, Hardwicke, no doubt to his eternal shame, was recorded by Mazher's sound man uttering the immortal words, 'Come on, bring on the Charlie! I want a big fat line. I'm going to have the biggest line I've had in my life and then be sick.'

The scooter deal, of course, was never completed, although the cocaine purchase was, all duly recorded and reported in the *News of the World*. Hardwicke was charged and the case came to trial at London's Blackfriars' Crown Court in September 1999 in front of Judge Timothy Pontius. Hardwicke's counsel, Alun Jones QC, put Mazher on the stand and subjected him to a thorough grilling. He quizzed him especially on his role in asking the Earl to supply him with cocaine.

Alun Jones: Is there a budget which the *News of the World* allocates for the purchase of drugs?

Mazher Mahmood: No, there isn't.

AJ: How do you get authorisation for the spending of money on cocaine?

MM: Well, there's no set budget, no, there isn't, but we need to ...

AJ: Do you have to get authorisation on any one occasion?

MM: No.

Judge Timothy Pontius: Petty cash?

MM: I don't think so. I probably paid for it myself and claimed it back. I'm not sure.

AJ: And you claim it back as expenses?

MM: Expenses, purchase of cocaine.

AJ: So are there documents for that for accounting purposes for the purchase of cocaine which go into the accounting system?

MM: Presumably, yes.

AJ: And auditors see that: 'For the purchase of cocaine', do they, of a public company?

MM: I assume so, yes.

AJ: Does Mr Murdoch approve of this activity?

MM: He obviously does, yes.

AJ: For you to go out and ...

MM: To buy cocaine.

AJ: Spend money to buy cocaine?

MM: That's correct, sure.

AJ: That is approved policy of the Murdoch press?

MM: That's correct. Absolutely. If it results in convictions I don't see what we're doing wrong. We're exposing criminals.

Mazher's defence was that if his investigative activities resulted in a criminal conviction of his target, then he was completely justified in buying drugs.

Roy Greenslade, commenting on the case in *The Guardian*, opined that Mazher Mahmood had effectively broken the law himself. Hardwicke's counsel, Alun Jones, pointed out after the case that the Misuse of Drugs Act makes 'no allowance for a private person to encourage another to supply drugs.' In other words, Mahmood himself broke the law. In mitigation for Hardwicke, Alun Jones also branded Mahmood 'an impulsive and malicious liar,' whose conduct involved 'serious breaches of criminal law.' He added, 'I submit that it is something that has to be examined more widely.' The jury's reaction was telling, too. They took seven hours and, although they found Hardwicke guilty, they passed a note to the judge that read: 'Had we been allowed to take the extreme provocation into account, we would undoubtedly have reached a different verdict.'

At the sentencing, the judge stated that without the jury's plea and the way the men were entrapped, they would have been looking at up to four years in jail. He told Hardwicke and Thwaites, 'Were it not for that elaborate sting you would not, I accept, have committed these particular offences.' He then gave the Earl a two year prison sentence and Thwaites fifteen months, both of which he then suspended for two years, so neither would serve any actual prison time.

Speaking for the PCC, Guy Black said subterfuge by reporters was acceptable only 'where they think it is in the public interest, if they are exposing crime, hypocrisy or protecting public health.'

Afterwards Mazher was roundly castigated, but, despite Alun Jones's submission, was never called to account for aiding and abetting his victims in their crime. It is remarkable, given the number of similar stings he has conducted in the decade or so since the Hardwicke case, that Mazher is still able to deploy the same tactics.

In the view of one experienced criminal barrister, in making funds available for their reporters to buy cocaine, Mazher, his bosses and the participating members of his team are committing the offence of conspiracy to possess a controlled drug. The motive of the person in possession isn't relevant and shouldn't be confused with his intention. In a case, for instance, where a police informer claimed as a defence that he had the drugs as a result of an arrangement with police officers to pass them onto another party who would sell them to an undercover officer (see R v. X [1994] Crim LR 827), the informer was convicted nevertheless, and the Court of Appeal dismissed his appeal.

That party responsible for supplying the funds to buy the drugs, which Mazher openly concedes was his employer, News International, had committed the offence of possession of a controlled drug as a secondary party, in that they aided, abetted or counselled him to possess the drug. A corporate entity could be prosecuted for this offence, as a limited company can, as a general rule, be indicted for criminal acts which must be performed by human agency and, in given circumstances, become the acts of the company. There is no obvious reason why News International should have any special immunity against prosecution for this.

Another of Mazher's cocaine sting victims was the popular BBC Radio 2 DJ, Johnnie Walker. In his recent autobiography, Johnnie describes how, on Saturday, April 24, 1999, he went home after a hard day's work, made himself some dinner and was relaxing at 11.00pm when his phone rang. One of his bosses, Trevor Dann, head of music at the BBC and in charge of output on Radio 2, was calling to tell Johnnie that he was on the front page of the *News of the World* and he'd better get out of town and hide himself away, because the rest of the press pack would be after him.

Johnnie couldn't take it all in. 'I'll need time to think,' he said. 'What about my Monday show?'

'You can take it that, as of now, you're suspended.'

Despairing, he recalled hearing a rumour that someone from the BBC was going to be fingered in a *News of the World* coke story, but Johnnie really hadn't thought he was a big enough star to merit the attention. After a sleepless night he snuck out in the morning to buy two copies of the *Screws* from his village newsagents. Only when he got back into his car, did he dare unfold the paper and look at the front page – to be greeted by a full-page photo of himself leaning over a mirror, snorting two enormous lines of cocaine! He stared at it and couldn't even associate himself with the face in the picture. He turned to the following pages to see a series of library shots of himself at various stages of his long, busy career, starting on Ronan O'Rahilly's pirate broadcasting ship, *Radio Caroline*. The report beside the pictures claimed that not only was he a regular user of cocaine, but he was also a dealer in the drug and a pimp who could arrange for prostitutes to come to parties. It could hardly have looked any worse, and though it was mostly rubbish, he knew he was in for a very rough ride.

And then he realised how it had happened. A few weeks earlier, a young exec from the *News of the World* had started pestering Johnnie about making a pilot for a monthly radio show to be played in the rooms of a chain of hotels owned by an Arab prince from the United Arab Emirates. Johnnie ignored the advances at first, but when they turned into a torrent of faxes, phone messages and emails, he decided the only way to put the guy off was to get in touch with him. Johnnie was told he was being offered two thousand pounds per show, plus a free holiday once a year in one of the prince's hotels. It sounded to Johnnie like a bit of a wind up, but in the end he agreed to make a pilot. A couple of weeks later, he heard that they liked it, and he had the job if he wanted it.

The next stage of the sting was a meeting at Sergio's restaurant with other members of the team. A western-suited, presumably Arab businessman introduced himself as the Emirates prince's UK representative. He handed over a heavily gilt business card and fiddled constantly with two mobile phones, one of which Johnnie realised later was a digital voice-recorder. He confirmed that his boss had agreed that Johnnie should be contracted to produce 12 shows per year, and they would like to meet him over lunch to get to know him. He agreed to a date at Claridges, and arrived there having had a couple of glasses of wine and – he admits – a quick line of cocaine to put himself, at least temporarily, on top of the world.

He was met in the foyer by the UK rep, who escorted him up to one of the most expensive suites. He did a quick double-take when he saw a vast, gold-toothed individual standing guard outside the door. It seemed too absurd to be phony, so he figured it was genuine. Inside the huge, sumptuous suite he was introduced to two Arab grandees in best-quality *djellabias*, smoking a huge hookah. Lavish in their welcome, they urged Johnnie to come to the Emirates as their guest. Then somewhat out of the blue, one of the sheikhs announced that he had a bad headache because he'd had some lousy cocaine the night before. Could Johnnie get them some better stuff? Johnnie was surprised, but he didn't sniff a set up. They pressed and pressed him, and in the end, to shut them up, he got out his own stash and cut some lines for them – and a couple for himself. The 'Arabs' said they'd save theirs until after they'd eaten. Johnnie shrugged, rolled up a £20 note and hoovered up his two lines, blissfully unaware that he was being photographed and videoed from several angles.

The sheikhs continued to pressure him to tell them where they could get more, and in the end, Johnnie succumbed. He gave them the number of a dealer he knew and told them to get on with it. To Johnnie, the whole business was getting a bit tacky and out of hand, even more so when they told him they were having a party the following Saturday and asked if he knew 'any girls who enjoy a good time who might like to come along.' Johnnie knew that the cocaine dealer whose number he'd already given them might be able to oblige, and suggested that they might contact him about the girls as well. At that the sheikhs announced they were going to change into suits for dinner, and Johnnie was taken back downstairs, feeling by now a little uncomfortable. He'd have felt a great deal more uncomfortable if he'd known that the cocaine he'd just given them was being swept up and sent off to a laboratory for testing.

Inevitably, the *News of the World* story implied that Johnnie had an arrangement with the dealer to send him punters for drugs and prostitutes in return for a big back-hander. Impossible to prove, of course, without hard evidence, but just as hard to disprove. They had poor old Johnnie banged to rights with the shots of his own snorting and let him have it with both barrels. And then the police entered the fray. At least they had the decency to admit that they were charging him because if they didn't, the absurdly sanctimonious *News of the World* would lambast them for being soft on drugs. Johnnie was charged with the possession of an amount of 0.06 grams – about a fiver's worth – and, more seriously, with intent to supply, which would carry a jail sentence in the unlikely event that it stuck.

After six months on tenterhooks – including a stint in rehab at Eric Clapton's Crossroads retreat in Antigua and a great deal of expensive lawyer's time – the "Intent to Supply" charge was dropped, presumably because it was unprovable. Johnnie appeared in front of a Horseferry Road Magistrate's court, was fined £2,000 for possession and allowed to go. It was great to be free, but Johnnie had been put through the mangle by Mazher Mahmood. In the meantime, no public interest had been served; no big dealer had been apprehended;

a great deal of money had been spent on police and court time in convicting a man for possession of 0.06 grams of cocaine. The payoff for the *News of the World?* Editor Phil Hall had sanctioned an estimated £50,000 budget, and a big splash with Mazher's by-line was on the front page again.

There's no question that for a long time, Mazher was considered a major asset by his bosses. What was and still is chilling is the fact that he smiles while he's sticking the knife in; he appears to be utterly unmoved as his victims' careers crash into the rocks (as, many insist, Mazher's own should have done for cheating at *The Sunday Times*.) Mahmood has always strongly defended himself against condemnation of his methods – as indeed have all the editors he has worked under – by pointing out the number of criminal convictions that have resulted from his exposés. With a characteristic *News of the World* cavalier approach to the facts, various comfortably round figures – 'Over 100', 'More than 200' – are suggested. His work, he has claimed in the course of several trials, has been praised by two home secretaries. Mazher's own scanty, poorly written and self-aggrandising website, set up by colleague Conrad Brown, currently claims 207 successful criminal prosecutions as a result of his work over the last two decades. Noticeably absent are figures for the years spent in jail by innocent men, the police hours wasted and the millions of taxpayers' pounds frittered away – all for the stings Mazher has constructed.

It would be fair to reiterate here that in his earlier days with the paper, Mazher did effectively expose an impressive number of genuine criminal activities and was responsible for fingering the culprits, leading to convictions that were clearly in the public interest. But over the years, even as the genuinely criminal has become less important to the paper, the Met and other police forces have still deemed it worth co-operating with the *News of the World* on the basis that it would be less risky to work with them than against them.

Up until now, Mazher Mahmood has had only one known serious falling out with the paper, reported by the Press Gazette in 2003. Following the fatal shooting of two Birmingham teenagers in

January 2003, Mazher Mahmood was assigned by assistant editor Greg Miskiw to go out and procure a gun for a story on how simple it was to buy hardcore firearms on British streets. Mazher made contact with a Yardie gang and went with Conrad Brown on a Friday to meet them in a Birmingham park. When Mazher asked to see the gun, it was put to his head, and five men in balaclavas appeared with guns and machetes. Mazher and his contact both received a 'severe kicking' and reportedly narrowly escaped a knifing by handing over all the money they had. Next morning while recovering at home, Mazher was phoned by Miskiw, who put him under intense pressure to get out and try again. Angry but indefatigable, Mazher phoned round the heaviest names in his book of contacts and that evening stormed into the newsroom at Wapping to dump a Kalashnikov AK47 on Miskiw's desk. His resentment was exacerbated when his finished piece was not only cut to a few paragraphs in a week when gun crime was dominating the rest of the media, but also ousted from the front page to make way for a lightweight *East Enders* buy up.

He and Brown resigned on the spot. By Tuesday they were reported back at work.

From time to time the Fake Sheikh has had his setbacks. Early in the 'Sheikh's' career, when he was standing around in an expensive London hotel, about to sting his next victim, someone strolled into the lobby, walked up to him and greeted him by his real name. It was David Yelland, then editor of *The Sun*, perhaps relishing the chance of a little friendly sabotage. Occasionally Mazher has nearly paid for not having taken the trouble to learn Arabic when he's been approached by other Middle Eastern potentates. Assuming he was one of their own, they have greeted him in their language, when he's had somehow to fluff his way out with a muttered 'A lekum, Salaam.' On another occasion, trying to trap a sergeant in a Guards regiment in a scam involving procurement of prostitutes, the soldier who had served in the Gulf, started speaking rapidly in Arabic to Mazher. The Fake Sheikh drew himself up while one of his aides explained, in English, that the Sheikh considered it rude not to be addressed in English while in England. More recently, he's shown a surprising lack of attention to detail by not doing enough homework on his targets' backgrounds or not adequately disguising his corporate identities and websites.

In addition, failures have been more common to some extent because Mazher's sheikh persona has been so widely reported that Mazher has become a victim of his own success. For instance, an image of him in fully sheikhly regalia has appeared and been widely circulated; it still appears on Mazher's entry in Wikipedia. The photo was taken at Nether Lypiatt, Gloucestershire home of Prince and Princess Michael of Kent. Mazher had come in his sheikh garb and trappings to inspect the house as it had recently been put on the market. Princess Michael, perhaps sensing an easy sale at a non-bargain price, was there to greet him as he landed in a helicopter the News of the World had hired for the trip. One of her party snapped the 'Sheikh' as he walked from the chopper. At the house and over a follow-up dinner at Claridges, he persuaded her to roundly traduce several members of the Royal Family, most notably describing the late Princess Diana as 'bitter', 'nasty' and a 'convenient womb'. She also indiscreetly opined that Camilla would be crowned Queen and that Prince Harry had a perfect right to wear swastikas if he wished. In his article, Mazher also alleged that she had used her royal connections to make money.

Princess Michael – as well as all those who deplored the subterfuge and entrapment that he'd got away with for so long – must have been cheered by news of the nailing of Mazher's 'Sheikh' by Respect MP George Galloway. In late February of 2006, the chief executive of the Islam Channel, Mohamed Ali, had informed George several times that an unnamed individual wished to meet him with a view to helping his Respect party and, less specifically, the 'community'.

George, given the polarity of his public image and his own admitted paranoia, was naturally wary of anyone bearing gifts and for a few weeks resisted the advance. However, coming under further, presumably convincing pressure from Mr Ali, he agreed to meet this putative benefactor on a Saturday evening after his weekly radio show on TalkSport.

His suspicions grew when he was told that the meeting would

take place over dinner at the Dorchester – too rich a place for a true supporter of a party like Respect.

George explained in an article he wrote on the Respect website how he'd arrived at the hotel in Park Lane to be met by Mr Ali and another man, possibly south Asian, whom he subsequently described as a slim, bald, elegant thirty-something, about 5'8" and wearing a well-tailored suit. They weren't introduced, but later the man handed him a card which announced that he was 'Sam Fernando', marketing director of a commercial organisation called the Falcon Group.

After 20 minutes, they were joined in the restaurant by another man who embraced George, once again without saying who he was, although later in the evening he told George that his name was Pervaiz Khan. He was a middle-aged, sleazy individual whose ethnicity George couldn't quite pin down, although he did note that neither of the men wore beards in the manner of devout Muslims, which they claimed to be. After a short, token attempt at small talk, the conversation quickly moved on to the business of blatantly offering George money. George was immediately sceptical when they asked, with no attempt at euphemism, if they could contribute to his election campaign, sponsor George as a Member of Parliament or fund his party.

George was unequivocal in his rejection, explaining that it was out of the question and, in any case, completely illegal for a UK political party to accept funding from foreign nationals. The men responded that if the funds were channelled through a British national, like Mr Ali, they could circumvent the law. George was adamant. It was just not possible, and he didn't want any part of it. If they wanted to help the 'community', they could invest in the Islam Channel or something similar.

Then the conversation took a bizarre turn: the men suddenly began talking offensively about Jews, bringing up what they evidently considered questionable aspects of the history of the Holocaust, along the revisionist lines of David Irving.

'You're not even allowed to quibble about the numbers,' the smooth-pated Sam Fernando averred. 'Not even to say it's five million!'

George had no inclination to go down that road, for while he is an outspoken critic of the State of Israel, he has never been an anti-Semite. 'David Irving isn't quibbling about numbers,' he said. 'In his heart he supports the Holocaust, which is the greatest crime in human history, and should be accepted as such.'

By midnight, George was more than ready to go.

Before he left, Pervaiz asked him if he would pose for a photograph with his chauffeur, who had seen George on television. The driver was sitting in the lobby and lumbered to his feet. He was an enormous man, made more menacing by a mouth full of gold teeth. When George asked him where he was from, he answered sparingly that he was from 'up north'.

As soon as George had left the Dorchester, he met up with his close associate Ron Mackay and told him at once that he thought he was being set up by the Fake Sheikh. He also rang Mohamed Ali to warn him that they might have been the targets of a *News of the World* sting. The appearance of the driver had fully confirmed George's suspicions. He recognised him easily from Andrew Marr's description in *My Trade* of 'Jaws', Mazher Mahmood's bodyguard, as well as Carole Caplin's description of him in a piece she'd written in the *Mail on Sunday* about Mazher's attempt to sting her:

'...a huge man, about 7ft tall, with gold teeth, thick lips and a bald head. Apparently some kind of bodyguard, he was straight out of a James Bond movie.'

Added to that was her description of the other individuals involved in her sting...

'Marcus da Silva, very dapper, very proper, and with an upright posture... a pleasant face, perfect skin and clear eyes,' who later introduced her to his boss, a man named, amazingly, 'Parvais' – identified by Caplin as Mazher Mahmood, although not in this case, posing as a sheikh, but as a Pakistan-based international businessman with interests in Dubai.

Galloway and Ron Mackay soon discovered that the Falcon Group's address, 64 Knightsbridge, was an accommodation office from which telephone calls and post could be automatically diverted. He also discovered that the same 'Sam Fernando' had attempted to subvert his former Parliamentary colleague Dianne Abbot in a fatuous, failed sting in 2004.

To add pungency to his revelations, he acquired and used the only known photograph of Mazher in full 'sheikh' gear – red-chequered head scarf, ghatra and billowing white *djellabia* – which was taken at Nether Lypiatt. George posted it on his busy website, along with a monochrome head shot from a fake Czech passport used by Mazher.

With bizarre self-righteousness, the *News of the World* sought an injunction to prevent the shot appearing, on the grounds that it would endanger Mahmood's life (not to say kill off the Fake Sheikh once and for all). But Galloway won, and *The Guardian* too published the photo, ignoring the *Screws* pleas. (Subsequently, though, the paper was granted its injunction and the picture disappeared from the web until it was posted on Wikipedia, which lies outside the jurisdiction of UK courts. A different picture of a casual, relaxed and long-haired Mazher Mahmood has since replaced the Sheikh shot on Wikipedia.) With his well-known sense of the theatrical, George went on splendidly to reveal every detail of Mahmood's cock-up, to a point where it seemed impossible that the Feikh of Araby could live to sting again. But as we've seen, he was not yet ready to hang up his *djellabia*, however shop-soiled, and he has struck several times since.

Even more gratifying than Galloway's lancing of Mazher Mahmood was one of the Fake Sheikh's most recent and most expensive failures. It first came to my attention in the most serendipitous way at 8.30am on Friday, September 28, 2007 as I was crouched, flash-fingered over my laptop in my regular roost at the Chelsea Arts Club.

My mobile rang; I saw it was my 19-year-old daughter, Alice. This was puzzling – a student of philosophy at Leeds University, she seldom rose before midday.

'Dad! Dad!' she said huskily. 'You're doing a book about the Fake Sheikh, aren't you?'

'Among other things,' I agreed.

'Well,' Alice went on breathlessly, 'a girl I know, Suze – she lives in a house with some friends of mine, I saw her last night and she said, "Is it your dad who's writing a book about the Fake Sheikh? Because I think he's trying to do a story about my boyfriend, Guy Pelly.".'

Alice has the inquiring mind of a budding writer and, no doubt also thinking of her father, she asked what had transpired. Suze said she couldn't really say much yet as Guy hadn't decided how he was going to deal with it and he was coming up to talk with her about it. But she also said he was absolutely certain he'd been set up by the Fake Sheikh.

I was, as a *Sun* hack might put it, 'gob-smacked'. It seemed too absurd that an individual whose activities I'd been studying and analysing over several months should have stubbed his toe on a friend of my teenage daughter's – and nobody else knew! At least, as far as I knew, nothing had been reported in any of the *Screws'* rivals or regular detractors. But then, I have often observed that such synchronicity becomes more common as one ages.

I asked Alice for more details; she said she'd get back to me once she'd heard what was happening. In the meantime, with a head start, I'd find out what I could for myself.

I was quite prepared to believe that Mazher Mahmood was involved, because 25-year-old Guy Pelly, long-standing friend of princes William and Harry, would have been a classic target for him. He is close to the princes, thought to be a little erratic and possibly susceptible to booze and naked women. Given Guy's reputation for keeping tight-lipped about his royal connections, the Fake Sheikh would have quite a scoop if he could succeed in getting him to spill some injudicious beans about Harry, or Charles and Camilla. Besides, there was always the chance that Pelly could be induced to offer some revelations about some famous, possibly royal, personage's use of recreational drugs.

Two days after Alice called me, a full page piece by-lined Katie Nicholl appeared in the *Mail* on Sunday, outlining what had happened, but without much detail and only a hint of the part played by the News of the World's infamous Fake Sheikh. A couple of weeks later, my daughter rang again.

Guy Pelly was part of Piers Adam's London nightclub empire. Originally Marketing Director, Guy was now partner in the Polynesian-themed Mahiki, which he'd made the hottest spot in town and which had become a regular hang-out for the young princes.

In mid-August a man calling himself Alex da Silva and speaking crisp, upper-crust English rang Guy and told him he had a business proposition to put to him. He asked if they could meet to discuss it; Guy agreed and da Silva turned up at Mahiki the next day. Da Silva appeared to be a well-turned out Sri Lankan in his late 30s. Short haired and pea-headed, he had a mouth like a cat's bottom, but was energetic and personable. He was, of course, none other than Kishan Athulathmudali (aka: Sam Fernando & Marcus da Silva), former employee of the Countess of Wessex's PR company, now Mazher Mahmood's highly successful 'roper'.

Swiftly and with his customary polish, he proposed that Guy go into business with the people he represented and set up a concierge company to franchise Mahiki in the US. He explained that there were substantial Middle Eastern funds available through a company belonging to his boss, an Emirates sheikh who owned property and construction companies. Now building hotels, the sheikh's company already had one up and running in Malaysia and were planning to build one in Las Vegas, which was where he hoped to put the first of the franchised Mahikis. He invited Guy to check out their website.

Guy told him he wasn't really interested – he had enough work to do on Mahiki in London. Da Silva pressed him and suggested that if he didn't want to come over himself to run the clubs, he might have a friend who'd like to get involved. Guy didn't feel there was anyone he wanted to recommend, and the meeting closed inconclusively. Over the next six weeks, da Silva phoned a few more times, urging Guy to rethink his position. In the end, he offered to fly Pelly and a friend first class to Las Vegas, where he could meet the prospective investor and look at the idea in more detail. Guy still wasn't at all interested in the proposition, and he couldn't think of anyone else who'd want to run a club in the States.

But, hey, he thought. What the hell! A first class trip to Vegas, the best roost and da Silva insisted that they'd have a great time – all paid for. Guy agreed to go and said he might bring his mate, entertaining and unpredictable party animal Tom Inskip. (Given the entertainment they were subsequently offered, it seems likely his hosts did indeed intend him to bring a male friend.) However, Guy changed his mind, and when he flew out from Heathrow on Friday, September 21, sitting with him in Virgin Upper Class seats was his girlfriend of over a year, Susannah Warren who, like Guy, was excited and looking forward to seeing Las Vegas. A lively, good-looking 19-year-old student at Leeds College of Music, she was the daughter of respected blood-stock agent, John Warren, and granddaughter of Lord Caernarvon, former racing manager to the Queen.

Guy and Susannah landed in Las Vegas around 3.00pm local time. They were met at the airport by 'Alex da Silva' in a limousine and rolled down the Strip past countless jumbotrons and blinking neon signs to the Bellagio, where they were installed in a large, glitzy suite. Once unpacked and settled in, they wondered what on earth they were doing there.

So far 'Alex', who said he was also in charge of the company's PR, was playing the genial host, entertaining and solicitous. Although Guy and Susannah were fairly wiped out by jetlag, they were asked to get ready to go out. Alex said his boss was waiting to meet them for dinner, so they were ushered back to the limo to be driven round to the Venetian. On the way Alex prepared them with a few jokes about his boss and how odd he might seem.

As they approached the suite a substantial bodyguard moved into place in front of the door. They were shown through into a massive suite where a butler and various assistants seemed busy, while across the room stood a handsome Arab in a wacky white silk Indian-style suit.

Alex introduced the 'Arab' as Mosin, the man who would be putting up all the money for the joint venture. Da Silva did most of the talking while his boss nodded quietly, joining in from time to time, not saying much.

They were lavishly entertained at dinner with a non-stop supply of drink. Towards the end, Mosin and Alex were talking between themselves, half-inviting Guy to join in, when Mosin glanced at Guy. 'What do you think of that Camilla? Don't you think she looks like a horse?'

Guy had learned to be on his guard for this kind of thing and wisely didn't react. Alex interjected, 'I'm so sorry,' he whispered apologetically. 'He's obsessed with famous people.'

'Weren't you at school with Prince William and Prince Harry?' Mosin pressed. 'You must know her.'

Guy was quite used to being pumped for information about the Royal Family by nosy people and journalists and offered his standard reply that he didn't have a view, as if he didn't know any of them. Since becoming a friend of Prince William and Prince Harry, Guy has always been loyal and over time has become well schooled in discretion about his royal mates. He'd taken a lot of the rap for the weed-smoking episodes a few years before, and despite having been offered huge amounts of money, he'd never muttered a word to anyone.

Alex and Mosin threw out a few other royal names, as if Guy might just chip in of his own accord, but now he was aware of a strong whiff of rat and carefully clammed up. When dinner was finally over, Guy told his host that he and Susannah were utterly knackered, and they would have to go back to their hotel. Mosin wished them good night, they were ushered out and Alex came with them in the limo back to the Bellagio.

The next day, Guy said that he and Susannah would like to have a look around the extraordinary, surreal resort on their own, which they did. In the evening they met up again with Alex who explained that Mosin wasn't going to be with them this time. Guy had already asked that he be shown around some of the best of the Vegas clubs, and they set out on a short tour. Now in geek mode, wearing his club-operator's hat, Guy was keen to examine the technicalities and was concentrating on that, when in one club, with the booze still flowing, Alex pointed out a man who'd just walked in.

'If you feel like some cocaine,' he said suggestively, 'that guy sells the best you can get round here.'

Guy and Susanna, puzzled by this unexpected reference to drugs, shrugged their shoulders and said they didn't use it. Da Silva, perhaps thinking they were just being reticent, pressed them. 'No really,' he said, 'that man has the very best. If you want some, he'll sell you whatever you like.'

Once again, Guy replied that they weren't interested, and Alex quickly dropped it. Guy suggested it might be fun to go to Spearmint

Rhino, one of the innumerable lap-dancing clubs that litter Las Vegas. Alex thought it a great idea and called up the limo to take them there. Throughout the evening, da Silva had been doing his utmost to make sure that his young guests were having booze poured down them as fast as possible, and they both admit to having been a little drunk by then.

Nevertheless, Susanna was finding the whole experience rather bizarre and thought maybe they'd been pretty foolish in coming. But not a great deal happened and she was prepared to see the funny side of Spearmint Rhino when the girls came up close and performed for them. Alex took a few pictures, and beyond that, nothing disgraceful took place. (In any event, there was a limit to what Guy would have done in a strip club with his girlfriend sitting beside him.) They were beginning to feel tired and a little uncomfortable and spent the rest of an awkward evening blanking questions, and wishing they could just go home. After that, not much more was said about the business proposition, and they went back to the Bellagio for the night. On Sunday morning, they had breakfast with da Silva and flew back to England in the afternoon, September 23.

By now Guy had grown more suspicious of the whole episode, and once they were back in London, the idea was beginning to harden that he had been a victim of some kind of stitch up. He had another look at Mosin's company's website, which posed several anomalies, not least that if you tried to contact them by email, the e-address came up as '@al-Jamal.com' (which George Galloway had found was registered at 233, Bethnal Green Road – the address of Ali Malik's Law centre). Guy's own research showed him that the site was registered to someone he'd never heard of – a Mazher Mahmood. He entered the name on Wikipedia, and up popped the information that Mazher Mahmood was a *News of the World* journalist, better known as the Fake Sheikh, and there, staring from the screen, was a good likeness of his proposed new business partner, 'Mosin'.

Guy was deeply incensed. He saw now exactly what they'd been trying to do. They'd gone out of their way to trip him up and he realised that if he'd just agreed to one of Mosin's derogatory statements about members of the Royal Family, Mahmood would have caught him and blazoned it across the front page of his paper. Guy's young career would have been ruined. He picked up the phone, rang the *News of the World* and asked to speak to the editor, Colin Myler, to complain about what he'd been subjected to. Myler replied that he knew nothing about it. Guy didn't believe him and decided to wait and see what the *News of the World* were going to do.

At the end of the week, Myler rang him, confirmed that it was indeed Mazher Mahmood that he'd met in Las Vegas, and they weren't running the story. In fact, they had no story – nothing beyond a few innocuous shots of Guy and Susannah at Spearmint Rhino. In the meantime, the *Mail on Sunday* had somehow got hold of the bare-bones of what had gone on in Las Vegas the weekend before and produced a carefully worded (and steeped in *schadenfreude*) exposé of the Fake Sheikh's failed sting, without actually naming Mazher Mahmood. Although Susannah's parents weren't too happy about it, no damage had been done, and the *Mail*'s piece wasn't such a bad result for Pelly. It was a nice coup for the *Mail* on Sunday and a good hard kick in the squishy organs for the Fake Sheikh.

Most pleasing to those who deplore Mazher Mahmood's activities was the abject failure of this sting, like his foiled attempt to subvert George Galloway the year before. And this time, Mahmood wasn't dealing with a seasoned politician, but a straightforward, blameless 25-year-old, who'd shown exemplary discretion and loyalty to his friends. The failure of Mazher's pathetic attempt at using his well-worn cocaine-buying ploy was pleasing too, and it is amusing to note that, as it was obvious that Guy couldn't have known where to get the drug in Las Vegas, it looked very much as if Mazher's team were prepared to be party to selling the stuff to Guy himself – a federal crime in the States.

What Mazher's editor Colin Myler had to say and what managing editor Stuart Kuttner felt about coughing up the tens of thousands the scam must have cost, with only a cringe-making piece in a rival paper to show for it, one can only imagine. But any hope that the collapse of this sting might have spelled the final demise of the Fake Sheikh was dashed only 2 weeks later when his team was back to its old tricks. Jodie Kidd was caught on camera allegedly admitting using drugs and arranging for one of Mahmood's team – Kishan again – to buy cocaine.

***

Mazher Mahmood himself remains a very enigmatic creature. When not in character as the 'Sheikh', he has always kept an extremely low profile. He is consciously unflashy and low-key, keeping himself to himself and making little effort to connect with colleagues on the paper, other than those on his team. He's not often seen around the Wapping newsroom, and when he does come in to see the editor or to sort out his considerable expenses, he doesn't hang about for the kind of gossip and banter that tends to flow there. Not surprisingly, he's had to keep up his guard after years of threats of revenge from people he's damaged, ever since a gang turned up wielding machetes at his parents' house in Selly Park. His father didn't approve when early on Mazher found stories within the community, because it isolated the family. At one point Mazher's betrayals even prompted a declaration by close family friends that they no longer wished to have anything to do with the Mahmoods. Nonetheless, his parents have always stood by him.

During his 17-year career on the *News of the World*, Mazher claims to have moved home several times as a result of death threats and has been beaten up more than once on undercover jobs. Letters and emails baying for his blood have arrived at the *News of the World*, and his own home is heavily protected. In 1999, when the threats became menacing, the paper agreed to pay for a personal bodyguard for Mazher, and he took on his second cousin, Qreshi to do the job. This was no mere act of nepotism, it was an obvious choice. Qreshi stands well over six feet tall and is built like a military blockhouse. It is he who over the years has been seen and described by several of Mazher's victims – Carol Caplin and George Galloway among others – as having an alarming set of solid gold teeth like the villain 'Jaws' who plagued James Bond over several movies. (Mazher must have made new arrangements since last year when Qreshi had to go, after a serious accident left him badly injured.)

The BBC's Andrew Marr is one of the few journalists to have interviewed Mahmood, for *My Trade*, his book on Fleet Street. The meeting took place in a secluded corner of a London hotel brasserie. Jaws was there, watching Marr's every move, and during the interview

Mahmood admitted that he'd spent much of his life watching his back.

'You soon get hardened,' he said, 'It makes you cynical... I find it hard to trust people... I have very few friends.' He went on to admit that his job, which earns him a rumoured £120,000 pa, has made him 'a bit of a pariah.'

It's the price he's paid for being the most notorious undercover reporter of his generation and, given the enemies he's made, one he'll go on paying for the rest of his life.

Since Mazher first came to prominence as an investigative journalist, his private life has remained a closed book. It turns out that, unexpectedly for a man engaged in a cynical profession, he seems in some respects to have behaved as a conventional Muslim son, agreeing to an arranged marriage with a girl whom his parents had chosen for him.

Nageen is the daughter of the vice-principal of the Open University in Pakistan and an old friend of Sultan Mahmood's. In 1990 she and Mazher were united in a lavish, traditional Muslim wedding ceremony held in Pakistan. They returned to England together, where the marriage lasted four months before breaking down in great acrimony.

Joining the *News of the World* in 1991, Mazher remained single again until 2001, when he remarried, this time to Sadaf, a young Pakistani studying in London, to whom he had been introduced by a friend – possibly his close associate, lawyer Ali Malik. After his second wedding, in Rawalpindi (at which Dr Malik is believed to have been best man and to which his brother Waseem was not invited), the couple returned to live in Mazher's Kensington house.

A son was born, but the second marriage, too, ended in messy divorce. Sadaf has remained in their Knightsbridge home, while Mazher has moved out amid wrangles over access to his child. Needless to say, details of these events are not readily available in the public domain, but the suggestion is that Mazher has found it so necessary to bury his own personality in obscurity that he finds it impossible to come out and live a normal life.

In the usual course of things, a journalist of Mazher's notoriety would be as visible as his former editor, Piers Morgan, or the late gossip king, Nigel Dempster, both of whom have often appeared on TV. For Mazher, guesting on Richard & Judy or GMTV and late night review programmes are simply not options. In addition to his anonymity, which is vital to his modus operandi, he has stung so many famous and often innocent people that he has become a deeply hated man. He is despised, too, not only by those in the Asian community, but also by fellow journalists. One veteran Red Top hack told me, 'Mazher's generally thought of as complete scum. He gives even tabloid journalists a bad name. What he practices you can't really call journalism.'

When speaking with Andrew Marr, Mazher was disingenuous. 'For me personally the best stories are the ones where we are rescuing kids or getting paedophiles banged up.'

Like any successful con man, Mazher has developed the ability to build other people's trust in him before abusing it without compunction. Reviewing the cuttings, it's clear that in his early days at the Screws, Mazher did focus on what might be called traditional Sunday tabloid targets – bent coppers, carousing firemen, corrupt county councillors, promiscuous vicars – all committing genuine acts of bad behaviour that their positions should have precluded. What has changed over the years, notably since Piers Morgan's appointment, is that the stories (and their entrapping set-ups) are now targeted almost exclusively at celebrities. The truth of a story is now a distant second to Mazher's unbridled ambition: his original crusading urge to right wrongs – so far as it ever existed – has been usurped by his unashamed need to see his by-line on front-page stories, regardless of their worth as items of public interest.

In fairness, it should be said that Mazher hasn't entirely given up pursuing stories of genuine and significant corruption when they're brought to him. As recently as December 2004, he exposed Tory councillor Suresh Kumar for demanding bungs for planning permission. No doubt it was an easier story to break for Mazher as a fellow British Asian than it would have been for a white journalist. He said as much himself in an interview with *Newsweek*, shortly after the Beckham kidnap farrago, 'It's the only reason I'm alive – because of my colour. Nobody would ever think I was a reporter. That's how you gain people's trust.'

But today the cynical generating of news-out-of-nothing that Mazher has been practising is long overdue a purge. There are signs that he's losing his touch and perhaps scrabbling around too vigorously. At the end of 2007, a rival tabloid gleefully reported a new misfire by the Fake Sheikh.

No doubt desperate to land a seriously high-profile target to make up for other recent failures, Mazher again set up a business sting, this time aimed at the once favourite tabloid royal target, Sarah, Duchess of York.

An email arrived at the offices of the duchess's New York PR people, purportedly from one Ivan Perera. 'Perera' wrote....

'I head up Aurelius Communications – which is the marketing arm of the Singapore based private equity firm, Emaar Capital. From our offices in London, we carry out the global marketing and PR activities on behalf of Emaar and its investment properties which are in a variety of industry sectors (won't bore you with all the background – probably better that you have a quick wander around the Emaar website when you get a few minutes).

'One area that Emaar is developing its investment portfolio in is with luxury brands and services, and to this end we are currently planning for the launch and brand development of Concordia – a personal assistant and concierge service. Concordia – can best be described as the ultimate in concierge and personal assistant services, and will be launching in 2008. We are at the moment, talking to a shortlist of candidates with a view to their participation in the marketing campaign for the launch, as well as to each one being taken on in the role of a consultant for the overall management in the first phase of the brand's activity. The Duchess of York is very much on this shortlist and all things being equal, we are very keen to start the ball rolling by way of an exploratory chat.'

This introduction was followed by a vague description of an implausible service being offered to broad spectrum of unlikely users....

Concordia will aim to provide the ultimate in wish fulfillment
for its clientele aged between 25 and 40, covering a 50:50 male:
female split, in the AB1 sector. Whilst each application for the
limited membership will be considered according to its merits,
prospective members will be expected to afford the annual five
figure annual [sic] subscription.

He went on to express a wish for the Duchess to become involved
in an advisory capacity, suggested a follow up chat and concluded
chummily...

I shall be more out of the office than in, in the next few days,
and with our inhabiting different time zones – my cell might may
[sic] well be the better bet, in order that we don't end up playing
telephone tag!

Kind regards
Ivan Perera
Aurelius Communications
London

This communication with its clumsy, pretentious PR jargon (plus ty-
pos) has all the hallmarks of Kishan Athulathmudali. (He'd at least
had the forethought to change his alias from 'da Silva' to 'Perera'.)

Mazher, with surprising and apparently increasing clumsiness,
had overlooked several things. For starters, Mazher had used the
name of a genuine and respectable Dubai-based property company called Emaar. Second, for some time the duchess has operated
a tight and profitable business and has gathered an able and savvy
team around her. Finally, she has gone a long way to reinstate herself
in the eyes of the public and would have been viewed sympatheti-
cally as a victim by a lot of *News of the World* readers. In any case,
it's a long time since she fell into any traps like this and it's hard to
imagine what indiscretions Mazher thought he was going to extract
from her by blundering in with his usual dodgy smoke and cracked
mirror performance.

His overeagerness reminds one of his former colleague, Clive

Goodman, who was forced to take desperate measures when he felt his position threatened.

Sarah's experienced staff weren't fooled for a moment by the amateurishness of the proposal or the alias names, companies and websites. They pulled the rug on the bumbling 'sheikh' and his dwindling team before they'd got to first base – a relief no doubt to Stuart Kuttner, who hadn't had to shell out too much of Murdoch's money before the scam aborted, and no doubt to the relief of editor Colin Myler, given his avowed, if somewhat tarnished public commitment in November 2007 to discontinuing the use of 'celebrity stings'.

When finally the hackneyed old coke-and-greed ploy has ceased to work at all and Stuart Kuttner no longer signs Mazher's expense cheques, when Tom Crone can no longer justify his support and Mazher is considered a spent force on the *Screws*, any newspaper in this country will be reluctant to touch him.

CHAPTER SEVEN

OF PUBLIC INTEREST VS OF INTEREST TO THE PUBLIC

For a year following his release on Monday, March 5, 2007 Clive Goodman dropped out of sight almost completely. After 37 days in custody, he left HM Prison Swaleside, on the Isle of Sheppey, wearing a 'Peckham Rolex' (an electronic tag to monitor his movements while on parole) around his ankle. He came out already knowing that he'd lost his job, because *News of the World* executives had rung Jennifer, his wife of 18 months, to inform her so. His former Putney residence had been sold to pay his legal costs, and Jennifer had moved home to a new address which they have so far managed to keep secret from all but their closest friends.

Soon after he left prison, a few friends took him to lunch in a London club for a 'Coming Out' party, but he couldn't stay too long; he had to be home for his curfew. At first Clive tried to make light of his experiences and joked that the prison cafeteria and News International's canteen must be run by the same caterers, but it was clear he wanted to lick his wounds in private, and those who saw him remarked on the deep gloom into which he'd descended. In the months that followed, he rarely went out, and he shunned all approaches for interviews, including repeated requests from *Tatler* editor Geordie Greig.

Rumours circulated around the industry that Goodman was seeking some kind of settlement for unfair dismissal by News International, although it's unlikely News International would agree to any settlement that could be construed as an admission of tacit complicity in Goodman's crime.

In May 2007, at the invitation of the *Sun*'s political writer Chris Buckland, Goodman made an appearance at a Press Gallery lunch at the Churchill Rooms in the House of Commons, at which Defence Secretary Des Browne was the guest of honour. He appeared again in October 2007, at the memorial service for his former boss, gossip supremo Nigel Dempster. There, Roy Greenslade asked him outright if he'd come to an arrangement with News International, but he refused to speak about it. Former colleagues describe him as looking shifty and evasive, while others say recent pressures had left him pale and drawn. Goodman is not without supporters; a number of his former colleagues have stood behind him. Phil Hall, James Whittaker, Deborah Lawrenson and Adam Helliker all declined to speak about him, on the grounds that Clive was a friend of theirs. It's to be expected that he wants to put the whole saga behind him, but his attempts to find employment elsewhere – perhaps freelancing for the *Mail*, or for his old friend and former colleague Adam Helliker on the *Sunday Express* have until very recently been fruitless. It looked very much as if his career as a journalist was over – a cruel blow to a man who'd spent over thirty years so utterly absorbed in his job – when in March 2008, one of Richard Desmond's newspapers found a slot for him.

In stark contrast, Clive Goodman's co-defendant Glenn Mulcaire treated his conviction and prison sentence 'like St Paul on the road to Damascus', as an AFC Wimbledon supporter put it.

Intelligent, ambitious, fiercely proud of his large family, Mulcaire was determined that he would come out of prison stronger than he'd gone in. He spent 11 weeks in jail, where inmates say he participated or instructed in every course on offer, which served both to teach him new skills and to make the time pass more quickly. It couldn't have been easy, seeing his wife and kids across the visiting-room table when they came to see him, watching them leave without him. He was, his supporters say, a man of principle, a diligent and committed father, and in the cold light of a prison dawn, he recognised that the events of the previous six months signalled a time for a new direction, a time to seek redemption for what he now realised were serious offences. He accepted that actions he might once have tried to justify were intrusive, unethical, immoral and, ultimately, against the law. He left HMP Ford knowing that he was coming out a new man.

After his release from jail, one of the first things Mulcaire did was to visit the football ground where he had spent some of the best days of his previous 5 years. Known there as 'Trigger' and the first player to score a goal for the newly formed club, Mulcaire was one of the leading lights and a local hero in what is still very much a community football club. At the Fans' Stadium off the Kingston Road in late December (AFC Wimbledon: 2, Carshalton Athletic: 0), the supporters were on the whole very forgiving, although several were clear that they wouldn't have been happy to have had their voicemail raided. They believed that Mulcaire's admission that he'd been seriously uncomfortable doing what he'd been asked to do by his bosses at News International, and that when the hand of the law finally grasped his collar, he was almost relieved, and prepared to accept that he had indeed transgressed. They pointed out too that given his uncertainty over the extent of illegality involved, Mulcaire had made no attempt to cover his actions. He had recorded his activities, with dates, contact numbers, passwords and PINs all logged in notebooks lying quite openly at his business premises and in his home.

In fighting his case, Glenn Mulcaire had also accumulated a great deal of new practical knowledge about the law, especially as it impinged on his activities, and in the associated areas of employment and libel law. He decided that this would form the basis of an entirely new career. He could use his mental agility and experience to gain valid professional recognition. With the necessary qualifications already in place, he enrolled on a degree course at the College of Law, Bloomsbury.

*

Glenn Mulcaire was by no means the only PI to have been engaged in the murkier practices of journalism, nor was the News of the World the only paper: he was simply the first to be caught and convicted under the terms of RIPA, and *News of the World* was his client. His sentence might to some extent have reflected the appearance at the end of 2006 of an important report entitled *What Price Privacy?* published by Richard Thomas. As Britain's first Information Commissioner, Thomas's statutory role was to promote public access to official information but more importantly to protect private information and data from unauthorised eyes. One section of the report – Operation Motorman – set out to show how much the 'dark arts' of investigative journalism were being practised, after being widely exposed in April 2005 at the trial of a well-known private investigator, Steve Whittamore.

Mr Whittamore, 56, and his colleague, 52-year-old John Boyall ran a successful private detective agency in New Milton, Hampshire, and were known to journalists from most of the national newspapers. Their well-established *modus operandi* relied on a chain of contacts through which information was passed. Typically, when Whittamore was rung by a journalist requesting information, he'd take down the details and ring Alan King, 58, a former policeman. King would then ring Paul Marshall, a 38-year-old civilian clerk whose work at a South London police station gave him access to the police database. Marshall would add the information requests to genuine enquires or crime reports and pass the results back to King, who would then ring Whittamore. Whittamore contacted the reporters and invoiced their paper for research services. Charges weren't low and conformed to a broad tariff. Simply to find an address cost £17.50; to obtain a criminal record, £500. Mobile telephone account details could cost anything up to £750.

As a result of Operation Motorman, enough evidence was accumulated to charge the parties involved with offences under the Data Protection Act. When the four men appeared at Blackfriars Crown Court in London, dozens of examples of information requests were revealed to the court. The private investigators were able to supply details of criminal records and other data from the Police National Computer, registered keepers of vehicles and driving licence details from the DVLA, ex-directory telephone numbers, itemised telephone billing and mobile phone records, and details of 'Friends and Family' phone numbers. None of this information could have been obtained legally by a private investigator. The detectives were participating in criminal activity to which, by extension, their clients, the journalists were party.

In addition to the ICO's Operation Motorman, previous investigations by the *Sunday Telegraph* in December 2002 had identified private detective agencies regularly tapping into private telephone calls for the tabloid press, and in January 2003, *The Times* reported the Inland Revenue's admission that some employees had sold confidential information from tax returns to outside agencies.

Among the numerous instances of information illegally obtained from Whittamore was the *Sunday Mirror*'s request for the criminal record of Jessie Wallace, the actress who played Kat Slater in *East Enders*.

On May 12, 2002 a story appeared in the paper, headlined:
"KAT'S GUILTY SECRETS.
She Hides Criminal Past from EastEnders Bosses"

On December 1, 2002, the *Sunday Mirror* ran an unkind and intrusive story about the death of Clifton Tomlinson, son of actor Ricky Tomlinson, which was made possible only through information passed on via Whittamore. Reporters requested salacious details of the life-style of the father of Jade Goody, the victorious *Big Brother* contestant who had become an irresistible tabloid target. Other requests for information included such trivialities as a check on the partner of 'EastEnders' actress Charlie Brooks and the driving convictions of a coach driver involved in a crash in France. One of the more bizarre inquiries was a call to check the number plate of a scooter which had been used to transport Bob Crow, the leader of the Rail, Maritime and Transport Union, during disruptions to the London Underground. This gave rise to a less-than-major story in the *Mail on Sunday* that when the Central Line had been closed due to a derailment at Chancery Lane, Crow had travelled to work on a scooter.

Victims of these invasions of privacy ranged from professional sportsmen and officials, TV and broadcasting personalities, and members of the Royal Household to people innocently (even innocuously) caught up with celebrity connections, for example, the mother of a man who'd once been the boyfriend of a *Big Brother* contestant, and the sister of the partner of a local politician.

Marshall and King pleaded guilty to conspiracy to commit misconduct in a public office, while Whittamore and Boyall pleaded guilty to a lesser charge of breaching the Data Protection Act 1998. All four defendants were sentenced by Judge John Samuels to two years' conditional discharge. Despite the leniency shown by the judge, the Whittamore case sent a shiver through the industry. Newspaper bosses had been aware of the case for some time before it came to court because journalists had been interviewed by the police during the investigation, though no charges had been brought against them. But those papers that had used Whittamore's services – and that was a majority of the nationals at one time or another – suddenly became very uncomfortable about being involved, albeit one remove away, in what was patently criminal activity. High-level meetings among executives were swiftly convened. Not surprisingly the court case and convictions went largely unreported by those same nationals, and there was a general feeling that things would quieten down, move on, and return to 'normal' in due course.

That was not to be.

Richard Thomas strongly believed that harsher custodial sentences for those found guilty of trading in personal details should replace the purely fiscal penalties currently in force, which prompted him to produce *What Price Privacy?* In it, Thomas included a league table showing the national newspapers for which Whittamore and his team had acted. Some had been involved in the court case, others had not, but Thomas gave details of the numbers of journalists and transactions involved at each newspaper.

The results made startling reading. That great upholder of honest, middle-class values, the *Daily Mail* came top of the league. 58 of its journalists carried out a total of 952 transactions (provoking some muffled sniggering among rival journalists). Second on the list was the *Sunday People*, with 802 transactions from 50 journalists. Forty-five reporters from the Daily Mirror had put in 681 requests. One journalist from the *Evening Standard* was involved in 130 transactions.

Not only the nefarious tabloids but most of the broadsheets made the table as well. *The Observer*, a consistent critic of tabloid malpractice, requested 103 items of information through four of its journalists. *The Sunday Times* had 52 transactions on the list, requested by seven hacks (although presumably these papers would have insisted that the stories they were pursuing were serious matters, not to be compared with tabloid tittle-tattle). The *News of the World* naturally featured, as did the *Sunday Mirror*. Even *Women's Own*, *Best* and *Closer* magazines used the services of the private investigators. It was also revealed in the report that in just one week in 2001, a journalist on a Sunday tabloid was billed for '13 occupant searches, two vehicle checks, one area search and two company searches', for a total bill of £707.50, plus VAT.

Richard Thomas's league table did not, however, paint a complete picture, for Whittamore's was only one among several agencies; other papers might have topped the league for other outfits. Secondly, it should be noted that most prosecutions for this kind of activity are brought under the Data Protection Act, and under section 55 (2) (d) of the Act, no offence is deemed to have been committed if a person can show that what they did was justified as being in the "public interest": if a paper is conducting an investigation into a fraud – an MP taking cash for questions, a paedophile ring or a gang plotting to assassinate the Prime Minister – its actions would be accepted as being in the public interest, and thus legitimate. The broadsheets can usually claim this defence, but the tabloids have a different agenda. Hard decisions should be made as to whether or not the private sex lives of footballers and TV soap actors are in the public interest, or merely "of interest to the public".

In an interview with the *Daily Telegraph*, Richard Thomas expressed the view that most of the information on the Whittamore list was 'tittle-tattle', and his underlying message was clear. While he did not name hacks on this occasion, he said, this practice should stop.

Following close on the heels of Goodman's and Mulcaire's guilty pleas, Thomas's report was published in December 2006, at which

Parliament, along with the serious media and a significant section of the public at large, loudly expressed their disgust at yet another reversion to bad practice among the tabloids. The pressure was on the nation's newspapers to clean up their act.

A source of irritation to many is the marked difference between the treatment of broadcast journalism and print journalism. Broadcasters have been regulated with increasing strictness in their approach to privacy over the last 20 years. The Broadcasting Complaints Commission (BCC), formed as a result of the 1981 Broadcasting Act, was replaced 1996 with the tougher Broadcasting Standards Commission (BSC). Chaired by ex-*Times* editor William Rees-Mogg, the BSC drew up and administered a code to avoid "unwarranted infringement of privacy in, or in connection with the obtaining of material" for radio and TV output. Most recently, as a result of the Communications Act, in 2003 the BSC was replaced by the Office of Communications (OFCOM), with statutory regulatory powers.

At one time, it was deemed that the comparative monopoly enjoyed by a very small number of broadcasters demanded greater restraints on the invasion of privacy than applied to our highly diverse press. Although this is no longer appropriate, given the massive choice of television now on offer, there is no great call for these restraints to be lifted to reflect the removal of that monopoly. There is now no reason why print journalists should claim 'freedom of information' as a defence any more than their broadcast colleagues. But out of a tradition that reflects the long history of an independent press in Britain, there has grown up a kind of sanctity around this freedom as it applies to the print media, a freedom which has been cited time and again in the arguments to resist the establishment of any statutory control over renegade papers.

The last two decades have seen two notable occasions when public outrage at the antics of 'Red Top' journalists has forced editors to review their position and make solemn promises to clean up their act or face legislation.

In 1988, at a memorial service for the popular TV broadcaster and presenter Russell Harty, the congregation included a number of leading figures from the media including Melvyn Bragg, David Frost, Ned Sherrin, Sue Lawley, Frank Muir, Lord Snowdon and John Birt, some of whom exercised considerable influence over public and official opinion. Harty's old friend, the playwright Alan Bennett, recognising the potency of his audience, rose to give the main panegyric. He used the opportunity to deliver a hard-hitting lambast at the tabloids, describing how they had ruthlessly hounded, raked, dug, exaggerated and sensationalised everything they could find about Harty's undisguised homosexuality.

They harassed anyone they could find in Harty's home village of Giggleswick, Bennett said, besieging his house, scouring his dustbins, chasing his car and forcing their way into the nearby public school where he had once been a master. As the relentless, horrible publicity carried on, jobs dried up for Harty, and he had to work hard at anything that came along. A year later, harassed, exhausted and suffering from hepatitis, Harty was raced to hospital in Leeds, where his consultant called a press conference to explain how seriously ill his patient was.

Bennett described the tabloids response:

'As he fought for his life, one newspaper took a flat opposite, and a camera with a long lens was trained on his ward. The nurse would point it out when you visited. A reporter posing as a junior doctor smuggled himself into the ward and demanded to see his notes. Every lunchtime, journalists took the hospital porters across the road to the pub, to bribe them into taking photographs of him.'

Another paper was so desperate to bring pictures and details of the dying man to their readers that one of its hacks despatched to another patient in intensive care a bouquet of flowers containing money as well as the phone number of the paper's Manchester news desk. (The flowers were intercepted by a nurse, and the hospital were restrained enough not to reveal which paper had sent them.)

Bennett went on, 'One saw in the tireless unremitting efforts of the team at St James' the best of which we are capable; and in the tireless and rather better rewarded efforts of the journalists, the worst.'

Even after Harty's death the vilification by *The Sun* became even more vicious, as the absence of a living victim removed the risk of libel.

The 'Red Tops' cruel treatment of Russell Harty was one among several gross excesses they committed that year. The *Sun*'s editor, Kelvin Mackenzie, in the face of outrage even from his own staff, ordered the publication of a photo of a woman – a devout Christian and a virgin – who had been brutally attacked and subjected to multiple rape. It had been tacitly agreed among all the papers never to identify rape victims (let alone publish pictures of them), but MacKenzie did it anyway, overlooking any legal implications, just to sell more papers. The Press Council condemned him for it; that was all they were empowered to do. Once again, he had crossed a boundary and got away with it.

At the same time, MPs were receiving more and more letters of protest which, along with massive jury settlements for libel in favour of Elton John and Sonia Sutcliffe, were strong indications that the public had had enough of gratuitous invasions of privacy. Shortly thereafter, the publication of pictures of dead and injured victims from the disastrous collapse of Sheffield Wednesday's Hillsborough stadium was the last straw and provoked more public anger.

The tabloid editors, realising they had to make some show of remorse, shuffled their feet, wrung their hands and promised not to do it again. But they were quietly confident that the dust would settle and that their pleas for retaining the principles of press freedom, in which they were supported by the serious papers, would always outtrump any public calls for legislation against abuses of privacy.

The Press Council, which was set up in 1953 to censure unacceptable journalistic conduct, had no quasi-legal status, rendering it a watchdog with no bite, and not much of a bark, either. As a result of the outcry in 1988, a private member's bill was introduced to the Commons aimed at setting up a statutory complaints body to deal with the press. It appeared to receive wide support and the Home Office responded by announcing that it would create a special committee to conduct a wide review of the press and deal with all the concerns raised by the invasion of privacy, including door-stepping, clandestine photography, persistent trick questioning and harassment of ordinary people at times of great distress. Taking over at the Home Office, David Mellor made his premature observation that the tabloid editors were 'drinking at the last chance saloon'.

Although the *Mirror* had vowed it would happen 'never again,' Mellor replied:

I think that's a relationship of sensationalism driven by the circulation war and throwing out of the window standards acceptable in a civilised society. I think it is in the public interest that there should be a free press in Britain. But what is of interest to the public is not always in the public interest. The fact that some people are morbid and curious about death and are morbidly preoccupied with other people's private lives is not a justification for it.... People have become almost in despair over some of the standards that prevail.

(This speech spawned a subsequent irony in that, having achieved no firm action as a result of his Home Office campaign, Mellor himself was unable to do anything a few years later to prevent all the embarrassing details of his affair with Antonia de Sancha from being plastered across the offending tabloid.)

As promised, in 1989 a new committee, chaired by David Calcutt QC, was set up to consider 'Privacy and Related Matters.' The recommendations of this respected committee were that the old Press Council should be replaced by a new Press Complaints Commission (PCC) which would have 18 months in which to show 'that non-statutory self-regulation can be made to work effectively. If it fails, we recommend that a statutory system for handling complaints be introduced.'

The press were required to set up the PCC among themselves, partially composed of serving national editors. Knowing when they were well off, they swiftly complied.

However, Calcutt's 1993 follow-up report on self-regulation was strongly critical of the PCC's performance. He recommended a complaints procedure administered by an independently constituted, statutory tribunal, as well as the establishment of a new offence (or 'tort') of Invasion of Privacy. In 1995 a Tory government white paper rejected these recommendations, and since the arrival of the Labour government, no plans for further statutory press regulation have been mooted.

Meanwhile, in the few years following their 1988 fall from grace, the tabloid press quickly reverted to its old tricks. In the early 1990s, as the Wales' marriage began to disintegrate, they licked their lips and dove in. Thanks to recent advances in technology, photographs could be easily doctored to suit an editor's taste. *The Sun* published shots of Princess Diana cavorting in a bedroom with James Hewitt, photos which appeared to have been taken with a telephoto lens through a country house window, but which turned out to be cleverly constructed hoax photos. Although the paper offered no justification for it, it was never punished. Not to be outdone, the *Mirror*, under Piers Morgan's editorship, is rumoured to have paid $250,000 for a shot of Diana and Dodi in a boat, in which Piers tells us (now a little regretfully) he ordered Dodi's head to be digitally turned through 180 degrees to make it appear that the two were kissing.

The next major crisis in public trust in the tabloids – a natural culmination of this unrelenting, contemptible press activity – was the deadly crash of the Mercedes under the Pont d'Alma.

In September 1997, the outrage, public and official, was furious, very loud and sustained. Commentator after commentator, politicians, serious editors, the public in their letters to the papers and to their MPs all condemned outright the grotesque paparazzi harassment of Diana and Dodi, which appeared to have led directly to their deaths. How could they do otherwise?

At Earl Spencer's powerfully articulated claim that they 'had blood on their hands', the tabloid chiefs hung their heads in shame.

'Never, never again!' they promised – again.

Legislation was mooted, again.

The sanctity of press freedom was invoked, again.

This time, the press cried, it would be different; the tabloid editors knew finally there was a line they could never, ever cross again. Hounding the Royals with paparazzi, and forcing their way into their private lives was strictly and for all time, off limits.

Until, of course a story occurred that was so hot it couldn't be ignored.

Even not so hot, ten years on... like the story of William's knee.

The aftershock of a national newspaper journalist being sent to jail has reverberated for many months. The PCC and the House of Commons Select Committee have both considered the affair in depth, and events have been minutely examined by other players in the industry. The debate over who ultimately was responsible rumbles on. The chief executive of News International, Les Hinton, was summoned by his master to cross the Atlantic, and the master's son, James Murdoch, is now the boss here. Change? We shall see. No clearly identifiable conclusions have been reached by anyone, and no changes to existing legislation have yet been proposed. The PCC stamped its foot, got jolly cross with the *News of the World* and issued them with a serious reprimand (though no specific punishment).

PCC Director Tim Toulmin maintains that the commission functions better by not being a quasi-legal body with the power to take evidence, pass judgement or mete out penalties. He cites, with some justification, the success they've had in curbing excessive paparazzi activity around Kate Middleton. But this is an exception, and one to which editors will adhere only as long as there's nothing too hot to miss. Besides, while it's possible to believe that this kind of gentlemen's agreement might once have functioned, ethical standards in journalism have fallen too far. It's not only Tony Blair who believes that the hacks have become 'feral beasts'.

It's almost possible to feel a little sympathy for our politicians, with so much pressure on them to defend their own private lives often forcing them to lie, if only to protect their own families from hurt and shame. And this is in a climate where, alongside the proliferation in television fakery and a general decline of accuracy in reporting (and in selling government policy, for that matter), a culture of dissemblance has grown up over the last dozen years on all sides – in Parliament from a string of philanderers having to lie about their private lives, to ministers responsible for producing the infamous 'Dodgy Dossier'.

After the upheaval at the *News of the World* in 2007, have the tabloids really taken note this time? On the face of it, for the time being, the majority of newspaper groups seem to have. Memos have been fired off banning the use of private detectives and warning journalists that management will no longer pay the bills. Private investigators cost newspapers huge amounts of money, so from that point of view, the bean counters must be breathing a collective sigh of relief. A number of tabloid journalists claim to have noticed a more cautious approach to editing since the Goodman case. Executives have been noticeably more wary when checking copy and ask more questions about the provenance of material, while editors are now prone to pulling stories if they sense that information may have been illegally obtained. But how long will it last?

Andy Coulson, who was by any assessment at the centre of this storm, will not proffer an answer. He has already moved a long way from these events. If his new boss, the Rt. Hon the Leader of the Opposition is lucky and Coulson's clearly demonstrated effectiveness continues, come 2010, the former editor of the *News of the World* might find himself right up there, hand in hand with a British Prime Minister – something even he couldn't have dreamed of sitting at his desk with his head on his arms at Beauchamps Comprehensive in Wickford.

Andy's spinning skills are manifest. His part in achieving the turn-round in David Cameron's prospects over the summer of 2007 is under-estimated by no one, and many believe he has moved closer to the middle of the Tory inner circle.

There is, though, an especially intriguing aspect to his already somewhat controversial appointment: the part played by the Shadow Chancellor, George 'Pretty Boy' Osborne. If you've been paying attention, you will recall that in 2005, Coulson ran a front-page splash on George, alleging that he had been involved with (like, been in the same room as) a small quantity of cocaine and a hooker. It was, as has been noted, a non-story, having originated 11 years earlier when George was 22, an age which excuses practically anything.

When the 'TOP TORY, COKE AND THE HOOKER' story appeared, I remember being struck not so much by the damage that might have been done to the ambitious and able young politician, but by how much good it had done him. After all, the story didn't say George himself had done anything at all. He hadn't snorted the coke, and he hadn't taken advantage of the hooker's professional skills, 'dominatrix' or otherwise. But it did make him look, by association, as if he'd lived a bit and had a touch of grubby humanity to him, which went a long way to counter his unsexy image of choir-boy-coiffed, Mr Goody-Two-Shoes.

In his well-constructed profile of Coulson in *The Guardian*, John Harris noted that Osborne and Coulson had 'got on well', even while discussing this 'exposé'. At the time the article was published, the people around George were, apparently, very worried, and George was said to have been suffering severe tummy rumbles and telling everyone how upset he was. Well, he would, wouldn't he? There'd be no point in constructing a subtle piece of well-spun double-bluff, then rushing about telling people how chuffed you were. For this astute act of spin, Andy established his credentials as a spinner with Osborne, and, at least covertly, made his political allegiance known. George and Andy were still in touch after Andy's resignation from the Screws. In fact, it was Osborne who suggested to his boss that Coulson might be just the man to give the white-tie-and-tails Tories some much-needed street cred among the elusive middle ground voters.

Piers Morgan, who gave Coulson his first Fleet Street job in 1988, was upbeat about the surprise appointment. 'Andy is one of the best journalists I have ever worked with. He's calm, focused, determined, loyal, charming, professional and hates losing. I expect him to grab Cameron's media presentation and give it the good kick up the junta it sorely needs. Don't be misled by the Essex accent: he's much smarter than the old Etonians he's about to work with.'

'Andy knows Rupert Murdoch very well,' said Phil Hall, friend and former News of the World editor. 'They have a good relationship, and Andy will bring that relationship to the Tories. He's also best friends with Rebekah Wade [of *The Sun*], and papers like that will be where the war is won.'

However people are still uncertain of his politics. He showed glimpses at the *News of the World* of being an instinctive Thatcherite, with hard right views on immigration and Law & Order. But editing a paper for Rupert Murdoch required him to support the Labour line chosen by the proprietor. In any event, Andy's background is in showbiz, not politics, and although he had dealings with a lot of politicians during his time as editor of the *News of the World*, it was not seen as his strong suit. Nevertheless, at this early stage, no one seriously doubts that he has a solid future as David Cameron's media minder, wherever that ultimately takes him. From the depths of depression and token disgrace, Andy has risen like a Michelin-starred soufflé.

Coulson's successor at the *News of the World*, Colin Myler, has yet to show, beyond the obligatory superficial noises, how affected he was by the public disgrace of his paper's reporter. His appointment seems to reflect the temporary need for a safe pair of hands in the Wapping hot seat. Despite a few opportunities for greatness, his career to date has not really sparkled and has already contained a few black moments.

Arriving in Fleet Street in 1974 at the age of 22 from a Southport news agency, Colin became a reporter at *The Sun* and the *Mail* and did well enough to be made news editor at the People and then Today when it was launched in 1985. Appointed editor at the *Sunday Mirror* for the first of two stints, he was at the centre of a huge privacy storm after the paper printed pictures of Princess Diana working out at her Chelsea gym. Nevertheless, he was promoted to editor of the *Daily Mirror* in 1994 only to be ousted a year later to make way for Piers Morgan.

A little disillusioned, Myler left journalism for a while, but the siren voices called him back to the editorship of the *Sunday Mirror* for a second time in 1998. Soon enough he stumbled into controversy once again. The paper ran an interview with the father of the alleged victim of a racist attack by Leeds United footballers Lee Bowyer and Jonathan Woodgate. The footballers' trial was still going on – indeed, the jury were out considering their verdict when the interview was published – forcing the judge to abort a costly trial. The paper was fined £75,000 for contempt of court, and Myler resigned.

Crossing the Atlantic, he joined Murdoch's New York Post, from which he was bounced back to London to replace Andy Coulson after

Goodman's jailing. One of his first acts as editor, suggesting at least some degree of corporate remorse, was to call in the PCC to address his staff on the Code of Practice. However, subsequent stories and their treatment suggest that not all of the staff took the PCC's words to heart. Under Myler's editorship a fresh Royal story was identified and blown out of all proportions to titillate the readers in the well-established Screws manner.

In June 2007 Prince Harry was away from his regiment, the Blues & Royals, on attachment to the British Army Training Unit, CFB Suffield, 150 miles southeast of Calgary, Canada. He'd been training hard with his men and, as is fairly normal for young soldiers, he wanted to unwind a little after a hard session. While on an R&R break in Calgary, he let his hormones take over and flirted enthusiastically with the lightly clad barmaids in the local Cowboy Club, getting to know them better when one of his fellow officers brought them back to the house they rented. One of the girls, Cherie Cymbalisty, sold her tale to the *News of the World* for £15,000.

The paper gleefully ran two stories packed with salacious detail provided by the girls he'd dallied with. It was more than indiscreet of him he realised when he saw the depth of coverage (although if he'd been 2nd Lieutenant John Smith, no one would have given the events a second thought). The *News of the World*, added their usual nasty sting by juxtaposing Harry's philandering with the fact that the 150th British soldier had just been killed in Basra – which was especially unfair, given that Harry himself had been aching to go to Iraq with his regiment and his men – as ultimately he did.

It came as little surprise to anyone a month later when it was reported in *The Ottawa Citizen* that the *News of the World* had tried to persuade Cherie Cymbalisty to record a phone call with Harry, which she'd refused to do. Under Canada's Personal Information Protection Act the recording of a phone conversation without the other party's permission is forbidden. It may well be that Cherie's refusal saved Myler's accident-prone career from yet another stumble.

CHAPTER EIGHT

WILL ANYTHING CHANGE?

My main purpose in writing this book is to encourage those whose function it is to oversee the workings of our national press to revisit the bases on which it is monitored and contained. There is a growing body of opinion that newspapers like the *News of the World* – by no means the only culprit – are out of control and unaccountable because those bodies and laws in place which define the 'Public Interest' and protect the privacy of both public and private individuals are manifestly too weak.

To some, the tabloids' cavalier attitude to the truth is axiomatic, but unimportant. In the words of a London cabby: 'The *News of the World?* It's a load of effin' crap... but it's a good laugh, innit?'

Not if you're a victim, it isn't. However fanciful, tabloid muck has a tendency to stick.

I am not a journalist, nor have I ever been; thus, as I pointed out in my foreword, I am not a member of the journalistic brotherhood that protects its fellows from one another. However, Nick Davies, an award-winning investigative writer on *The Guardian*, has broken ranks, and chosen not to comply with the tacit understanding that journalists even from opposite poles of the industry do not foul each other's doorsteps. In *Flat Earth News*, he presents a thorough examination of press slovenliness and malpractice in journalism amounting to an endemic criminality which in any other profession would be brought to face criminal prosecution.

In a Radio 4 Today interview, Davies was arrogantly rubbished by *News of the World* managing editor Stuart Kuttner, who has been responsible for payments to investigation agencies and PIs like Glenn Mulcaire for years. He claimed Davies's well-researched analysis was 'totally unrecognisable'. 'If it happens, it shouldn't,' he said. 'It happened once at the *News of the World* and the reporter went to prison,' he added self-righteously.

The kid-glove treatment of Andy Coulson after the Goodman case points up clearly that there is no public watchdog sufficiently strong to mete out chastisement in a way that will seriously hurt and therefore deter the rest. For while the House of Commons Select Committee on Culture, Media and Sport castigated the Press Complaints Commission for not bringing Coulson in for questioning (on the flimsy basis that he had left the industry and no longer fell within their jurisdiction), neither did the Committee didn't call him in, when they clearly had the right to do so. Meanwhile, Coulson has gone on to occupy what could, in time, be an important governmental function.

The Guardian's reaction to the PCC's findings on May 18, the day its report was published, offers a succinct summary of the whole affair:

> The Press Complaints Commission has effectively cleared the *News of the World* of any illegal conspiracy in the Clive Goodman royal phone-hacking scandal.
> There was "no evidence" that anyone else at the paper was aware of Goodman's illegal activities, the PCC said today as it concluded its investigation into the affair, which saw the jailing of Goodman, the paper's former royal editor.
> 'There is no evidence to challenge [editor] Mr Myler's assertion that: Goodman had deceived his employer in order to obtain cash to pay Mulcaire; that he had concealed the identity of the source of information on royal stories; and that no one else at the *News of the World* knew that Messrs Goodman and Mulcaire were tapping phone messages for stories,' the PCC said.
> However, the PCC did criticise the News International tabloid,

saying its internal controls were 'clearly inadequate'.

The PCC also issued six new recommendations on undercover newsgathering and compliance with its code of practice.

It said it found 'numerous examples of good practice throughout the industry, both as regards the code of practice and the Data Protection Act'.

The PCC added that Mr Myler had improved internal controls at the paper since taking over, including more robust contracts of employment with staff members and external contributors.

Mr Myler told the PCC that the Goodman episode represented "an exceptional and unhappy event in the 163-year history of the *News of the World*, involving one journalist".

He emphasised the newspaper's commitment to the code of practice and said another unnamed reporter had been dismissed for breaching its terms.

During the court case the *News of the World* admitted that it paid Mulcaire a retainer of £104,988 per annum. The court also heard that he had received £12,300 in cash from Goodman.

Mr Myler told the PCC that the paper had paid Mulcaire, a former Wimbledon footballer, for 'legal and legitimate' work.

This included fact gathering, suggesting strategies, credit status checks, Land Registry checks, directorship searches and analysis of businesses and individuals.

Other activities Mulcaire carried out for the *News of the World* included tracing individuals from virtually no biographical details, date of birth searches, electoral roll searches and checks through databases; County Court searches and analysis of court records, surveillance, specialist crime advice and professional football knowledge.

There had been a 'great deal of inaccurate media speculation' concerning this contract, Mr Myler said.

Goodman also paid Mulcaire £12,300 in what the *News of the World* said was a 'direct and personal relationship'.

The paper told the PCC that Goodman deceived his employers by disguising Mulcaire's identity. Goodman claimed that the payments were for a confidential source on royal stories, identified only as 'Alexander'.

'The identity of that source and the fact that the arrangement involved illegally accessing telephone voicemails was completely unknown and, indeed, deliberately concealed from all at the *News of the World,*' the paper said.

'It was made clear at the sentencing hearing that both the prosecution and the judge accepted that,' Mr Myler told the PCC.

Mr Myler also told the PCC that the Goodman case appeared to have been a 'rogue exception' and that the News of the World ordered external contributors to abide by the watchdog's code and the law.

Following Goodman's conviction, Mr Myler he had emailed every member of staff individually, and written to them at home, with the PCC code of practice.

News of the World staff had been informed of a new clause in their contracts that said failure to comply with the code of practice could result in summary dismissal.

Goodman is suing News International for unfair dismissal.

Although it had been alleged as early as March 2007 that Goodman was launching a claim against News International for unfair dismissal, since then no case has been brought to court, which is puzzling. He was on the face of it unemployable by any national newspaper, and in view of the circumstances and lack of due diligence on the part of his employers, he could be seen to have a good case. The offer of a job on Richard Desmond's *Daily Star Sunday* came as a great surprise to many. In any case, although they have reluctantly admitted 'ultimate responsibility' through Andy Coulson, the *News of the World* would surely be wary of any kind of private settlement lest that imply complicity in a proven crime.

Six months after expressing his reassurances before the PCC, Colin Myler suggested that he would be urging his journalists, specifically Mazher Mahmood, to ease off producing tales of celebrities taking drugs and misbehaving. Speaking at the Society of Editors Conference on November 5, 2007, he stated, 'I think there are other issues that he [Mahmood] should be looking at – issues that affect the fabric of society, and we will see a bit more of that.' Myler had scarcely time to take his tongue from his check when, within two weeks of his avowed new direction, Mazher's lead story was the Sophie Anderton cocaine and sex-for-sale romp. Mr Myler's promises do not inspire great hope.

How assured can we feel by his boss, Rupert Murdoch, who, when asked on a News Corporation results call if there was adequate protection in place to prevent another Goodman-style scandal, replied, 'Absolutely. Every newspaper is making a very close examination of how they are operating'? To *Media Guardian* Murdoch said, 'If you're talking about illegal tapping by a private investigator, that is not part of our culture anywhere in the world, least of all in Britain.'

Although it's impossible to know how many times *News of the World* bosses tacitly condoned questionable investigatory techniques through their 'need not to know', there's no question that the paper used the services of Whittamore and Boydall. According to Richard Thomas's 'Operation Motorman' schedule, 23 journalists from the *News of the World* put through 228 transactions.

In March 2003, *Sun* editor Rebekah Wade had been called along with several other editors to give evidence to the Commons Select Committee for Culture, Media and Sport. In response to a question from Labour MP, Chris Bryant, she admitted, 'We have paid the police for information in the past.'

When Bryant asked if it would happen again in the future, her then-colleague Andy Coulson interjected, 'We have always operated within the (PCC) code and within the law, and if there is a clear public interest, then we will.'

The MP pointed out that it was against the law for police to be paid for information. Later he added, 'If newspapers are suborning police officers, encouraging them to think that there is money to be made from selling information, that can only be bad news for the criminal justice system.'

More recently, in September 2007 (3 months before announcing that his son James was taking control of the UK operation) Rupert Murdoch was questioned by members of the UK House of Lords Communications Committee who had flown to the US as part of their inquiry into Media Ownership and the News. Murdoch took the opportunity to outline his editorial approach as it affects his British papers. He explained insouciantly that 'the law' prevented him from instructing editors of *The Times* and *The Sunday Times*. The independent board put in place as a condition at the time of his purchase of the papers was there to make sure he couldn't interfere. Or say, 'do this or that'. Murdoch claimed, though, that he often asked, 'What's going on?', but the evidence suggests he was being disingenuous.

Robert Thomson, former editor at *The Times* and now Publisher of the *Wall Street Journal*, was quizzed over this by Roy Greenslade on BBC Radio. He firmly declared that his proprietor never directly instructed him on editorial matters. But it's more than likely that Murdoch makes his agenda very clear before appointing editors, and they know what will happen if they don't adhere to it – making direct intervention unnecessary.

Murdoch's first editor at *The Times*, Harold Evans, was sacked for holding political views at odds with his own, and the paper swiftly lost its former balance, becoming a partisan organ that strongly supported Margaret Thatcher. In fact, during its first nearly 200 years, *The Times* had 12 editors. Murdoch hired and fired 5 in his first 11 years.

Simon Jenkins, fresh from his seat on the Calcutt committee in 1990, was one of Murdoch's more unusual appointments as editor. Massive debts in the early days of Sky TV were preoccupying News Corps, and Jenkins was hired for tactical reasons, to fight off the threat of the burgeoning *Independent*. He certainly didn't share Murdoch's political stance, but for the next two years, Murdoch largely left him alone, apart from occasionally ringing up to tell him that he'd produced 'a fucking awful front page.'

Of his UK tabloid titles Murdoch described himself to the Lords Communications Committee as a 'traditional proprietor', exercising editorial control on major issues such as Britain's place in Europe and which party to back in a general election. The truth is that his ownership allows him to set the agenda of the papers and maintain the cultural thinking and ethos behind them.

Not unexpectedly, this is downplayed by his tabloid editors. In January 2008, *Sun* editor Rebekah Wade appeared before the Lords committee in London, where she assured their lordships that, far from Murdoch telling her what to do, he had never 'discussed tomorrow's newspaper in the censorious sense that you keep telling me exists and I say doesn't'.

She had, she said, not backed down when he'd complained to her about the excessive coverage she was giving *Big Brother* – often four or more pages at a time. One can believe he might have told her he didn't care for *Big Brother* as entertainment – a position held by many of us – but given how well Fox TV has done with its reality shows in the US, he must have understood the fascination these shows hold for readers of *The Sun*. Perhaps he's just disappointed that BB isn't broadcast by Sky.

In any case, the wide perception that Ms Wade was talking through her auburn curls was given support by reformed ex-Murdoch-lackey Andrew Neill, who also appeared before the committee and roundly rubbished her evidence. 'If you want to known what Mr Murdoch really thinks,' he advised, 'read the editorials in *The Sun* and the *New York Post* because he is editor-in-chief of these papers.' Neill, who used to edit *The Sunday Times*, added, 'When I was there, the editor of *The Sun* would get daily telephone calls.'

Regular inspection of Murdoch's UK tabloids reveals no sign that he has abandoned the tactics he deployed in Australia in the 1950s on papers such as the *Perth Sunday Times*, which he quickly bounced into profit by having it concentrate on scandal, showbiz gossip and sport, just as it does today.

However, in his single-minded support of the sometimes viciously intrusive prurience of his most popular papers, Murdoch presents something of a paradox. The assumption is that there must be a connection between the personal moral stance of an individual and the direction in which he or she steers a powerful means of influence under his or her control.

Murdoch has been characterised as an arch-villain for decades by a growing number of Murdochophobes, a group which draws from all sections of the political spectrum and includes disgruntled ex-employees, commercial opponents, politicians, celebrities, sportsmen, entertainers and ordinary members of the public whose lives have been damaged by one or other of the Murdoch papers. Add to these an army of disgusted ex-readers. Those who work for Murdoch titles are in no doubt about the angles they should take and the perspectives they should ignore. A former reporter on *The Australian* describes Murdoch editors as 'terrorists in suits... showing all the signs of being anti-intellectual and homophobic.'

Some of his tabloid editors have also understood that the ability to instil fear in the staff is one of the most efficient tools in the management armoury: it dispels the need to back up instructions with tedious, time-consuming explanations. Although this must engender little trust or loyalty among the staff, those who are committed to the Murdoch ethos can remain loyal, until they fall foul of him.

The more one looks at Murdoch, the more one sees his many contradictions. He is the newspaper proprietor most highly rated by his peers and competitors. His charm is legendary, and he possesses extraordinary ability to remember names and personal details, or at least, to operate a very efficient aide-memoire. His courtesy to his employees is often remarked upon. Bruce Page, a former (pre-Murdoch) *Sunday Times* journalist writes in his 2003 book, *The Murdoch Archipelago*, "Rupert is a very kind man personally. He bailed out old war correspondents who have hit hard times. He has great charm, in a certain dry way."

Murdoch's devotion to his family and his healthy relationships with his four children are well-documented. He certainly seems to have been and to be today a genuine, hands-on father and grandfather. He is not flashy, nor is he known to be a vulgar spender, residence in Beverly Hills aside. His former regular attendance at church and a substantial contribution to the building of a new Catholic cathedral in Los Angeles demonstrate that he is prepared at least to concede the possible existence of a power mightier than himself (always endearing in a major tycoon).

Many aspects of the man's character could lead one to the conclusion that Murdoch is a decent, rational man, who simply wants to make a success of his business in the way he knows best, and who employs tens of thousands of people with whom it is said he shares a reciprocal loyalty. But too often, Murdoch's actions prove otherwise.

He has a reputation for loathing the British establishment, as witnessed by his cavalier demeanour when a guest at the Queen's Golden Jubilee celebrations, during which he appeared deeply uninterested and chatted on his mobile. He is said to resent the hereditary aspects of monarchy, and yet in the running of his business, he has been as fervently nepotistic as any Saudi prince. Murdoch inherited his first newspaper from his father, and he has since given his sons and daughters various powerful positions within News International, culminating in his appointment of James as his principal CEO.

He justified this in an interview with Bill Hagerty in British Journalism Review in 1999...

> 'I certainly haven't lived my life the way I have without wanting to keep opportunities open for my children. I think that's natural. They've got to work, and they've got to prove that they can do it, which a Royal Family doesn't have to do.'
> Former insider Andrew Neill observes, 'The signal it sends out is that no matter how good you are, if you haven't got the Murdoch genes, you won't get the top job.'

Murdoch still knows when and how to turn on the charm. Nicholas Coleridge, who as far as I know has never been beholden to Murdoch, aimed at an even-handed approach in the portrait of Murdoch that appeared in his 1993 appraisal of the world's newspaper proprietors, *Paper Tigers*. He describes meeting the great tycoon: 'Rather like one's first sight of the Taj Mahal, there is a slight feeling of disappointment on first seeing Rupert Murdoch, that he isn't bigger.' Coleridge paints a picture of a considerate man who, although he can get quite tetchy, in real life seems to defy the Beelzebub portrayals.

I haven't met Rupert Murdoch; perhaps I should have in the interests of balance in this book. Coleridge (and others) certainly convey that he's good and entertaining company for a few hours. But I didn't want to risk being seduced, as others have been, by his charismatic charm. For it is near impossible to reconcile his image as a doting father and a good and thoughtful man with the permanent flow of invective, personal damage and vile rumour and the propagation of tawdry titillation and baseless fear in the readers of his *News of the*

World – for which he is ultimately responsible. Certainly he is capable of hypocrisy: Murdoch has often been quoted saying the British people are 'anti-success' and bluntly criticizes them for dragging down their heroes – this from the man who funded and condoned an all-out character assassination of well-loved triumphant British rugby captain and sporting icon, Lawrence Dallaglio.

More broadly, there is not even the pretence of balanced reporting in political stories (insofar as they appear at all) in the *News of the World.* Murdoch frequently makes it clear in his own statements that he has a distinct political agenda to promote. He would claim, as others have done in the past, that it is the prerogative of unelected media bosses to use their own platforms to promote whatever views they hold. That may, perhaps regrettably, be so, but in Murdoch's case, a major cause for concern is the manner in which he seduces readers whom he seeks to influence using his callous disregard for individual privacy, which he cynically wraps in claims of operating in the public interest.

***

When I sought recommendations for what should be done to bring the wayward sectors of the British press back into line I was presented with a wide range of views. Tim Toulmin at the PCC maintains that the patchwork approach currently in place, with "the law having an important role to play in relation to news gathering as well as publication of confidential information, and the PCC policing professional standards over and above these requirements and getting quick remedies for people when they need them" is about right. He goes on to say that the concepts of 'privacy' and 'public interest' are best left as fluid as possible, so that they can be interpreted according to the circumstance of the case, how much material is in the public domain, the complicity of the individual concerned and their behaviour, while at the same time leaving room for changing social expectations and standards.

There are admirable instances where this approach to monitoring the press does work, and undoubtedly it would all the time, were all newspapers edited by saints and sages. The brutal reality is that policing is effective only when there is recourse to a means of effective chastisement. What laws there are have proved too lenient to deter transgression.

Max Clifford, the most potent publicist in Britain, is a practical man. He suggests that proactive (rather than reactive) decisions should be made about actions involving invasion of privacy by a journalist while pursuing an investigation in the public interest. A journalist should know the rules before the intrusion occurs, rather than after the event, when any damage will already have been done, irrespective of an absence of public interest and any compensation a victim might subsequently have been paid. This would require the establishment of a panel possessing and wielding utter discretion, to which an editor or journalist must apply before the bins are raided, clandestine photos taken, phones tapped, or emails hacked into. Obviously the constitution of such a panel would have to protect the privacy of journalists and their investigations, as well. This is a practical suggestion which wouldn't compromise the privilege of Press Freedom, but would induce potentially wayward editors to think harder before abusing that privilege.

Another proposal is that those papers that abuse the rights accorded them under the auspices of Press Freedom should be punished by having those rights removed for a period of time. They would lose the right to claim 'public interest' as a defence for any intrusion of privacy whatsoever, and would be punishable in a meaningful way for any subsequent transgressions – including the prevention of an offending editor or journalist from working in that capacity, either for a period of time, or in extreme cases, forever.

John Whittingdale, chairman of the Commons Select Committee for Culture, Media and Sport, has considered that the PCC should be able to impose on seriously errant editors a day's suspension of publication, which would hit them hard, and very publicly, in the wallet. There are parallels for this at the British Horse Racing Board, which is able to chastise those within its jurisdiction by restricting their activities.

Perhaps a freshly constituted and more circumspect PCC should be granted powers to award and set compensation for victims from transgressors, which would also offer the possibility of redress for private individuals without funds to take a libel case to court. Along with these measures there is strong case for looking more closely at payment for information. Information sold to newspapers by people who, through their work or through relationship, have privileged access to details of an individual's private life should be restricted to cases where the individual has been involved in illegal activity.

Furthermore, the prevalent practice of buying pictures of celebrities taking and/or buying illegal drugs has created a market for such transactions. In this, and in the well-recorded instances of Mazher Mahmood buying drugs, News International, a British Plc, has been directly involved in aiding and abetting criminal activity and should be called to account by its share-holders.

Measures like these require, above all, a clear definition of the right to personal privacy, which is not statutorily available in this country. Elsewhere this is more clearly defined. The French Civil Code provides that 'everyone has the right to respect for his or her private life'. To protect 'the intimacy of private life' a court can make an interlocutory order directing whatever steps may be necessary to put a stop to violations of this right. The notion of 'private life' has been developed through case law by the French courts, which have held that 'a person's private life includes his or her love life, friendships, family circumstances, leisure activities, political opinions, trade union or religious affiliation and state of health.' The contention that a strong interpretation of 'privacy' would in some way emasculate freedom of press expression is not borne out by practices in France, where despite a legal delineation of personal privacy, publications such as *Le Canard Enchainé* are quite capable of damning journalism – when it is clearly justified, as opposed to merely gratuitous.

More simply, the invasion of privacy could be defined as the publishing of information regarding those aspects of an individual's personal life – sexual relationships, marriage, family, children, health, hobbies, religion – which have no demonstrable bearing on any public position they might hold, when no statutory offence has been committed.

Despite the absence of such definition in the UK, Information Commissioner Richard Thomas has been wholehearted in grasping this thorny issue and has shown a more muscular approach than the PCC to the protection of private information.

Thomas has emerged as the principal champion of personal privacy in this country. In What Price Privacy? he points out that respect for privacy is one of the cornerstones of the modern democratic state. The European Convention on Human Rights declares:

'Everyone has the right to respect for his private and family life, his home and his correspondence.'

'Failure to respect an individual's privacy can lead to distress and in certain circumstances can cause that individual real damage, mentally, physically and financially. Privacy is in itself a value that needs protecting, even when the loss suffered is not readily quantifiable in terms of damage and distress.'

In an ICO survey, 'Protecting people's personal information' came third in respondents' lists of social concerns, ranking only behind 'preventing crime' and 'improving standards in education'. The same report suggests that, while a fair balance must be struck between allowing journalists to do their job in pursuing genuine investigations clearly in the public interest, and protecting individual privacy, the PCC should take a much stronger line in tackling press involvement in the illegal trade of personal information and images. For their part, the Information Commissioner's Office declared, it would not hesitate to take action in the future against any journalist identified in the Whittamore investigation who is suspected of committing an offence.

The ICO has been vigorous in its attempts to seal the breach in laws protecting privacy and, recognising the inexorable growth in data theft, has demanded that the penalty for offences under Section 55 of the Data Protection Act 1998 – currently fines of up to £5,000 in a Magistrates' court, and unlimited in the Crown Court – be raised to a maximum of two years imprisonment. A clause to this effect, Clause 76 was embedded in the current Criminal Justice and Immigration Bill. It was progressing through both houses of

Parliament, and looked to be well on its way until April '08, when, after heavy lobbying by the press, including a strong presence from News International, a shameful, compromising fudge was agreed by Downing Street.

The clause would be put on the statute book, but then suspended, with the option for the Justice Secretary to invoke it at some future date. The precise status of a suspended clause is obscure and the muddy waters stirred up by this last minute government U-turn make it unclear in what circumstances its invocation could be triggered – if at all without Parliamentary consent.

Richard Thomas, who fought so hard for this new legislation, has been frankly snubbed. Despite all of the work he has done and the evidence he has unearthed, the threat of imprisonment – which would have been a far more effective deterrent to stealing private data than a mere fine – has been neutered.

***

Every survey and report on the subject over the last 20 years shows that gross intrusion by the *News of the World* and other tabloids into the private lives of celebrities, of ordinary people who have found themselves on the front pages through no act of their own and of the Royal Family, has grown to excessive levels.

But, along with the cynical role of the tabloid editors and their journalists, there is also a part played by the public – and a surprisingly broad sector of it – in this wholesale trade in personal privacy. While some 85% of the British population can get through Sunday without opening a *News of the World* there is a significant 15% who, apparently choose to immerse themselves in the prurient, exaggerated and sometimes downright fictitious accounts of the private lives of even the most implausible celebrities. Even I will admit to having, very occasionally, succumbed to buying a copy of the *News of the World*, but with the same furtive feelings of guilt and self-disgust that eating a Big Mac might evoke. It's a nasty habit which reflects badly on all who participate, and gives Britain a bad name. It's time we learned to accept that what politicians, princes, sporstpersons and entertainers do in public is our business; what they do in private is theirs.

Despite the promises issued every few years by editors and executives of offending newspapers that they will cease, the scale and depth of their intrusion has increased, aided and abetted by continual improvements in surveillance technology. To the layman it's clear that changes in the law must be made. But ranged against any such proposal are the editors' cries that nothing should stand in the way of Press Freedom. Most fair-minded people understand this, too – up to a point. However, one of the formidable obstacles to change is the symbiotic relationship between the Press and our National Legislature, as shown by the recent sidelining of Clause 76. For too long Parliament has been wary of upsetting editors and their powerful proprietors – especially Rupert Murdoch – and, faced with a united front across the range of newspapers on the matter of Press Freedom, they have, so far, been dangerously cautious in their approach to the problem. But now, with the force of genuine public opinion behind them, it's time for our legislators to show the necessary courage.

Our representatives in government are there to reflect the views of voters, not proprietors of newspapers and, while arguments in favour of a totally Free Fourth Estate are potent and complex, a means of dealing with the rogue players, the persistent perpetrators and the downright chancers among the tabloid editors must be put in place before the right to a private life in the United Kingdom has disappeared completely.

The End

I am grateful for the information I sourced in the following publications:

Max Clifford, *Read All About It*, Virgin Books (2005)
Gerry Brown, *Exposed!*, Virgin Books (1995)
Charles Wintour, *The Rise and Fall of Fleet Street*, Hutchinson (1989)
Matthew Engel, *Tickle the Public*, Phoenix (1997)
Piers Morgan, *The Insider*, Ebury Press (2005)
Chris Horrie, *Tabloid Nation*, Andre Deutsch (2003)
Johnnie Walker, *The Autobiography*, Michael Joseph (2007)
David Walsh & Lawrence Dallaglio, *It's in the Blood*, Headline (2007)
Andrew Marr, *My Trade*, Macmillan (2004)
Peter Chippindale & Chris Horrie, *Stick it up your Punter*, Pocket Books (1999)
Waseem Mahmood, *Good Morning Afghanistan*, Eye Books (2007)
Nicholas Coleridge, *Paper Tigers*, William Heinemann (2003)
Simon Jenkins, *The Market for Glory*, Faber & Faber (1986)
Tom Watt & David Beckham, *David Beckham: My Side*

And to:
The British Library, Colindale.
The Press Complaints Commision
The Information Commissioiner's Office
The House of Commons Select Committee for Culture, Media & Sport.

'Our greatest fear is not that we are inadequate, our greatest fear is that we are powerful beyond measure. By shining your light, you subconsciously give permission to others to shine theirs.'
Nelson Mandela

Travel can be a liberating experience. As it was for me in 1990, when I was just one hundred yards from Nelson Mandela as he was released from prison. I watched this monumental occasion from on top of a traffic light, amidst a sea of enthralled onlookers.

This was the 'green light' moment that inspired the creation of Eye Books. From the chaos of that day arose an appreciation of the opportunities that the world around us offers, and the desire within me to shine a light for those whose reaction to opportunity is 'can't and don't'.

Our world has been built on dreams, but the drive is often diluted by the corporate and commercial interests offering to live those dreams for us, through celebrity culture and the increasing mechanisation and automation of our lives. Inspiration comes now from those who live outside our daily routines, from those who challenge the way we see things.

Eye Books was born to tell the stories of 'ordinary' people doing 'extraordinary' things. With no experience of publishing, or the constraints that the book 'industry' imposes, Eye Books created a genre of publishing to champion those who live out their dreams.

Ten years on, and sixty stories later, Eye Books has the same ethos. We believe that ethical publishing matters. It is not about just trying to make a quick hit, it is about publishing the stories that affect our lives and the lives of others positively. We publish the books we believe will shine a light on the lives of some and enlighten the lives of many for years to come.

Join us in the community of Eye Books, and share the power these stories evoke.
Dan Hiscocks
Founder and Publisher

eye books

At Eye Books we are constantly challenging the way we see things and do things. But we cannot do this alone. To that end we have created an online club, a community, where members can inspire and be inspired, share knowledge and exchange ideas.

www.eye-books.com

eye**Community**

Membership is free, and you can join by visiting www.eye-books.com, where you will be able to find:

What we publish
Books that truly inspire, by people who have given their all, triumphed over adversity, lived their lives to the full.

Visit the dedicated microsites we have for each of our books online.

Why we publish
To champion those 'ordinary' people doing extraordinary things. The real celebrities of our world who tell stories that celebrate life to the full, not just for 15 minutes.

Books where fact is more compelling than fiction.

How we publish
Eye Books is committed to ethical publishing. Many of our books feature and campaign for various good causes and charities.

We try to minimise our carbon footprint in the manufacturing and distribution of our books.

Who we publish
Many, indeed most of our authors have never written a book before. Many start as readers and club members. If you feel strongly that you have a book in you, and it is a book that is experience driven, inspirational and life affirming, visit the 'How to Become an Author' page on our website. We are always open to new authors.

www.eye-books.com

eye**Community**

Eye-Books.com Club is an ever evolving community, as it should be, and benefits from all that our members contribute.

eye-**Books Club** membership offers you:

eye-**News** – a regular emailed newsletter of events in our community.

Special offers and discounts on the books we publish.

Invitations to book launches, signings and author talks.

Correspond with Eye Books authors, directly. About writing, about their books, or about trips you may be planning.

Each month, we receive enquiries from people who have read our books, entered our competitions or heard of us through the media or from friends, people who have a common desire – to make a difference with their lives, however big or small, and to extend the boundaries of everyday life and to learn from others' experiences.

The Eye Books Club is here to support our members, and we want to encourage you to participate. As we all know, the more you put into life, the more you get out of it.

Eye Books membership is free, and it's easy to sign up.

Visit our website: www.eye-books.com

Registration takes less than a minute.

www.eye-books.com

eyeBookshelf

THE AMERICAS / ASIA

	Thunder & Sunshine · Alastair Humphreys	The Good Life · Dorian Amos	The Good Life Gets Better · Dorian Amos	Cry From the Highest Mountain · Tess Burrows	Riding the Outlaw Trail · Simon Casson & Richard Adamson	Trail of Visions Route 2 · Vicki Couchman	Riding with Ghosts · Gwen Maka	Riding with Ghosts – South of the Border · Gwen Maka	Lost Lands Forgotten Stories · Alexandra Pratt	Frigid Women · Sue & Victoria Riches	Touching Tibet · Niema Ash	First Contact · Mark Anstice	Tea for Two · Polly Benge	Baghdad Business School · Heyrick Bond Gunning
eyeThinker		●	●	●		●		●	●		●	●	●	●
eyeAdventurer	●	●	●		●		●	●	●	●		●	●	●
eyeQuirky						●								
eyeCyclist	●					●						●		
eyeRambler														
eyeGift	●											●		
eyeSpiritual														

THE AMERICAS										ASIA			

AFRICA / EUROPE

	Moods of Future Joys · Alastair Humphreys	Green Oranges on Lion Mountain · Emily Joy	Zohra's Ladder · Pamela Windo	Walking Away · Charlotte Metcalf	Changing the World from the inside out · Michael Meegan	All Will Be Well · Michael Meegan	Seeking Sanctuary · Hilda Reilly	Crap Cycle Lanes · Captain Crunchnutz	50 Quirky Bike Rides...in England and Wales · Rob Ainsley	On the Wall with Hadrian · Bob Bibby	Special Offa · Bob Bibby	The European Job · Jonathan Booth	Fateful Beauty · Natalie Hodgson	Slow Winter · Alex Hickman
eyeThinker		●	●	●	●	●				●				●
eyeAdventurer	●	●										●	●	
eyeQuirky							●	●			●	●		
eyeCyclist	●						●	●						
eyeRambler									●	●				
eyeGift	●						●	●						
eyeSpiritual					●	●								

AFRICA							EUROPE						

eyeBookshelf

ASIA / AUS

Categories: eyeThinker · eyeAdventurer · eyeQuirky · eyeCyclist · eyeRambler · eyeGift · eyeSpiritual

Book / Author	Thinker	Adventurer	Quirky	Cyclist	Rambler	Gift	Spiritual
Travels in Outback Australia — *Andrew Stevenson* (AUS)	●	●					
Last of the Nomads — *W J Peasley* (AUS)	●	●					
Prickly Pears of Palestine — *Hilda Reilly*	●						
Jasmine and Arnica — *Nicola Naylor*	●	●					
Good Morning Afghanistan — *Waseem Mahmood*	●	●					
Behind the Veil — *Lydia Laube*		●					
Siberian Dreams — *Andy Home*	●	●					
The Jungle Beat — *Roy Follows*	●	●					
My Journey with a Remarkable Tree — *Ken Finn*	●						
Fever Tress of Borneo — *Mark Eveleigh*		●					
Desert Governess — *Phyllis Ellis*			●				
Trail of Visions — *Vicki Couchman*	●	●					
Jungle Janes — *Peter Burden*		●				●	

EUROPE / CROSS CONTINENT

Categories: eyeThinker · eyeAdventurer · eyeQuirky · eyeCyclist · eyeRambler · eyeGift · eyeSpiritual

Book / Author	Thinker	Adventurer	Quirky	Cyclist	Rambler	Gift	Spiritual
More Traveller's Tales from Heaven and Hell — *Various*			●			●	
Further Traveller's Tales from Heaven and Hell — *Various*			●			●	
Traveller's Tales from Heaven and Hell — *Various*			●			●	
Blood Sweat and Charity — *Nick Stanhope*		●					
Triumph Around the World — *Robbie Marshall*		●				●	
Great Sects — *Adam Hume Kelly*	●						
Discovery Road — *Tim Garratt & Andy Brown*		●					
Death — *Herbie Brennan*	●						
Around the World with 1000 Birds — *Russell Boyman*		●				●	
Travels with my Daughter — *Niema Ash*	●		●	●		●	
Forensics Handbook — *Pete Moore*							
Con Artist Handbook — *Joel Levy* (EUROPE)		●				●	
The Accidental Optimist's Guide to Life — *Emily Joy* (EUROPE)	●	●					

eyeBookshelf

Good Morning Afghanistan

by Waseem Mahmood
£16.99

"Good Morning Afghanistan was an important start in bringing fast and uncensored information to the war-stricken people of Afghanistan. The radio has served the realisation of freedom of speech and democracy for our country."

President Hamid Karzai
Islamic Republic of Afghanistan

After the fall of the Taliban, as soon as Kabul was liberated, came a radio station with a mission. This is the true story of how a broken nation finds a voice through the radio and learns to live, to be happy, to listen to music and to laugh.

Following the events of 9/11 Waseem Mahmood helped to set up and operate Afghanistan's first free radio station. Good Morning Afghanistan is the unique account of what Waseem and his colleagues achieved in the chaos that followed the overthrow of the Taliban. Gun-toting US marines, roaming gangs of Afghan fighters and a total lack of electricity and equipment are just the most immediate hurdles facing the intrepid team.

This is the story of how a broken nation finds a voice through the radio. Over the airwaves a land ravaged by decades of war learns again what it means to live, to be happy, to listen to music, to laugh and be joyful at all life's colours.

Good Morning Afghanistan is a fast-paced mix of humour, bathos and heartbreak that breathes life into the dry news bulletins that accompanied the fall of the Taliban regime. The reader is assaulted with the sights, sounds and above all the smells of downtown Kabul in the months that followed the US invasion.

Waseem Mahmoud is the brother of the News of the World's Fake Sheikh and in this best-selling account uses media as a positive influence tio rebuild lives as opposed to destroying them.